copyright © 2020, Erwachsene Malbuch

von

Meditation Malbuchverlag

alle rechte vorbehalten.

Die Vorschauseite

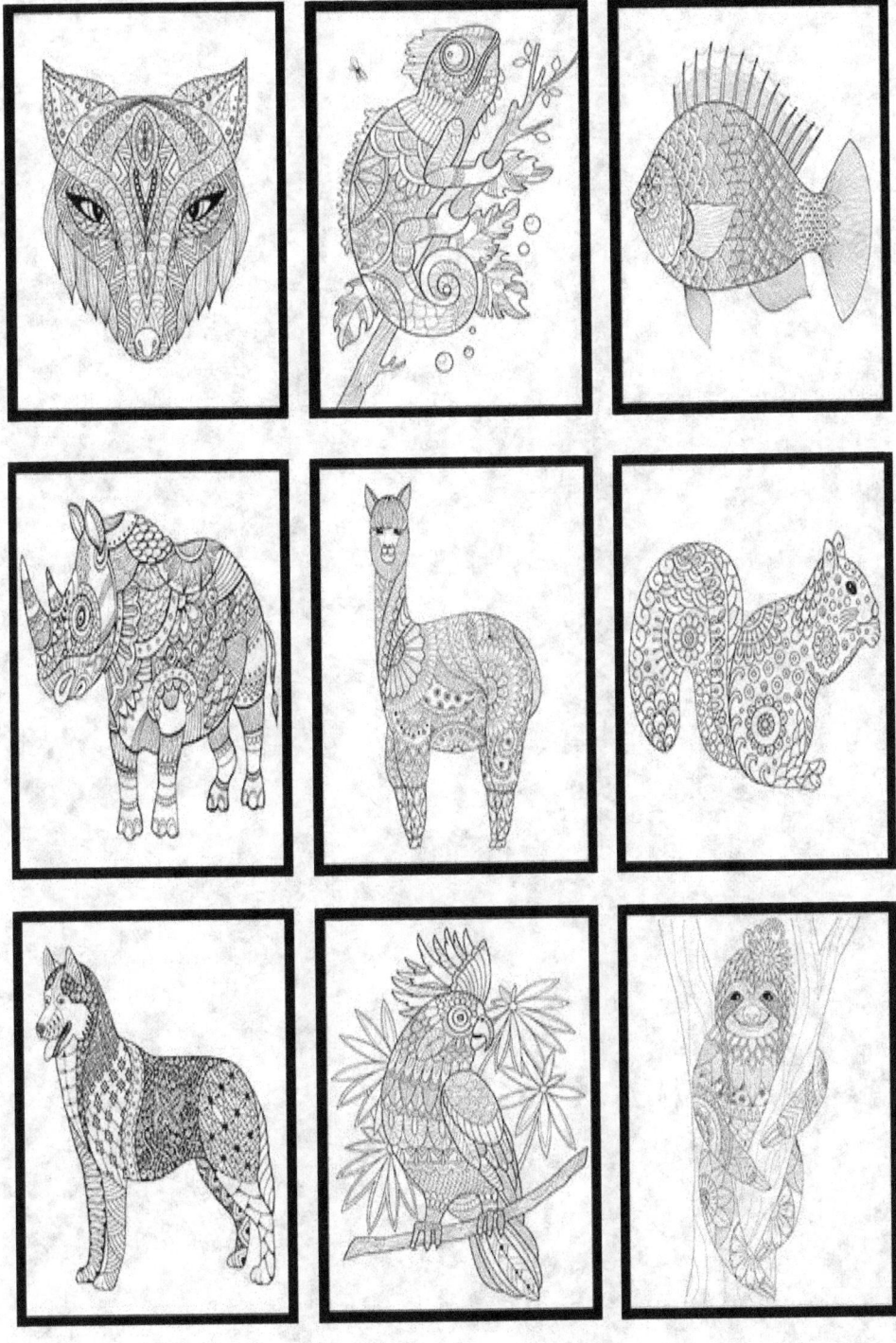

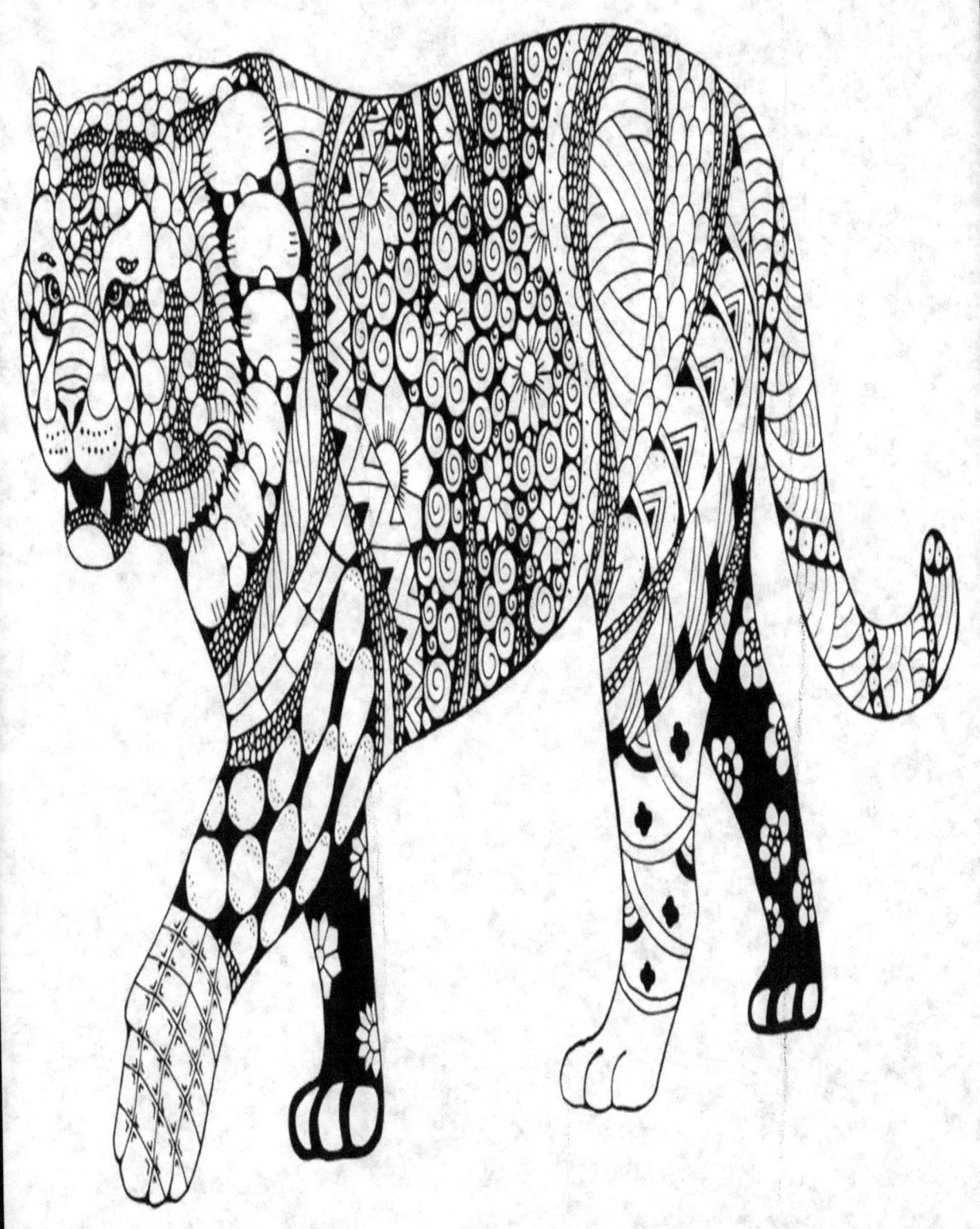

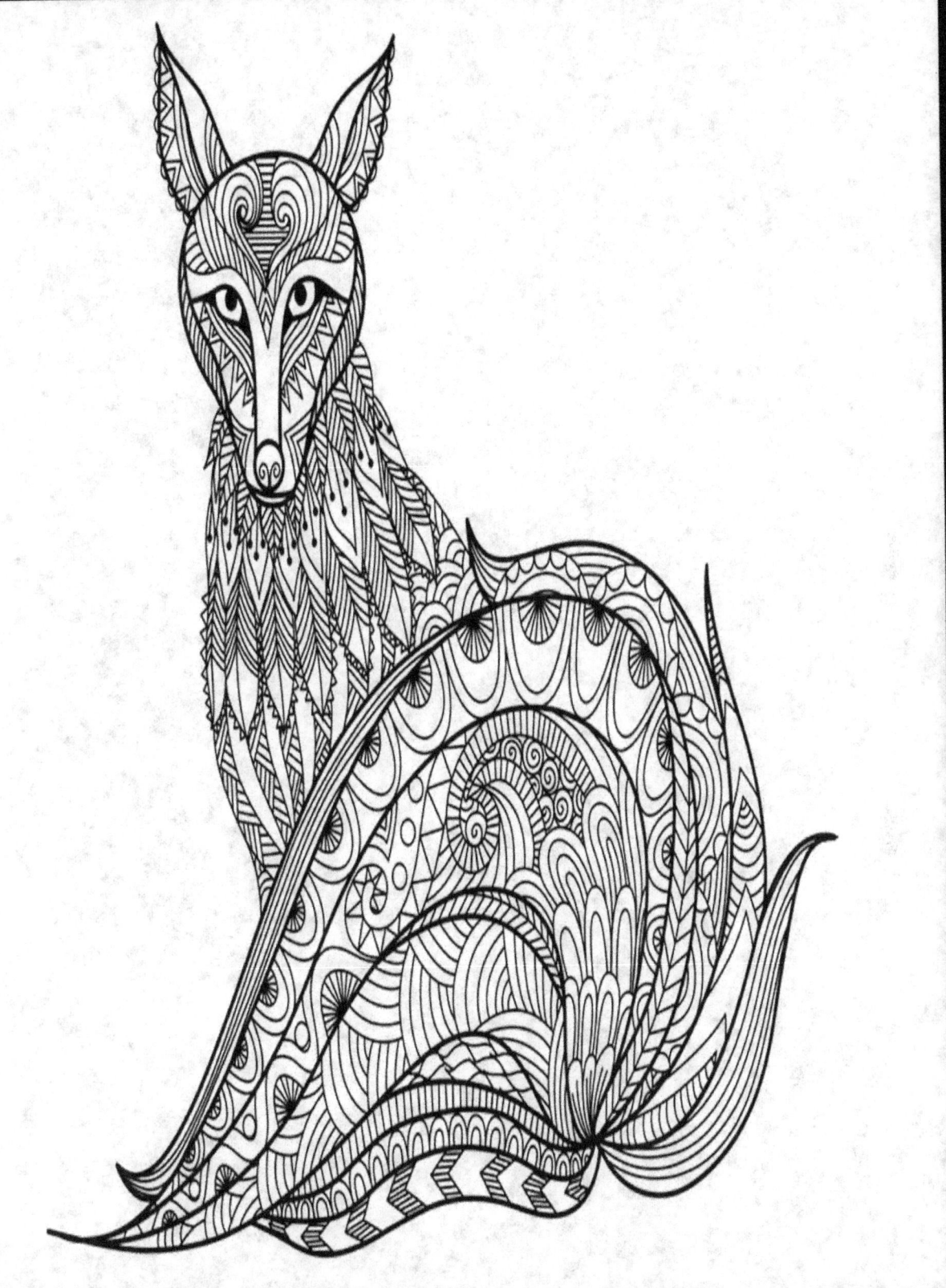

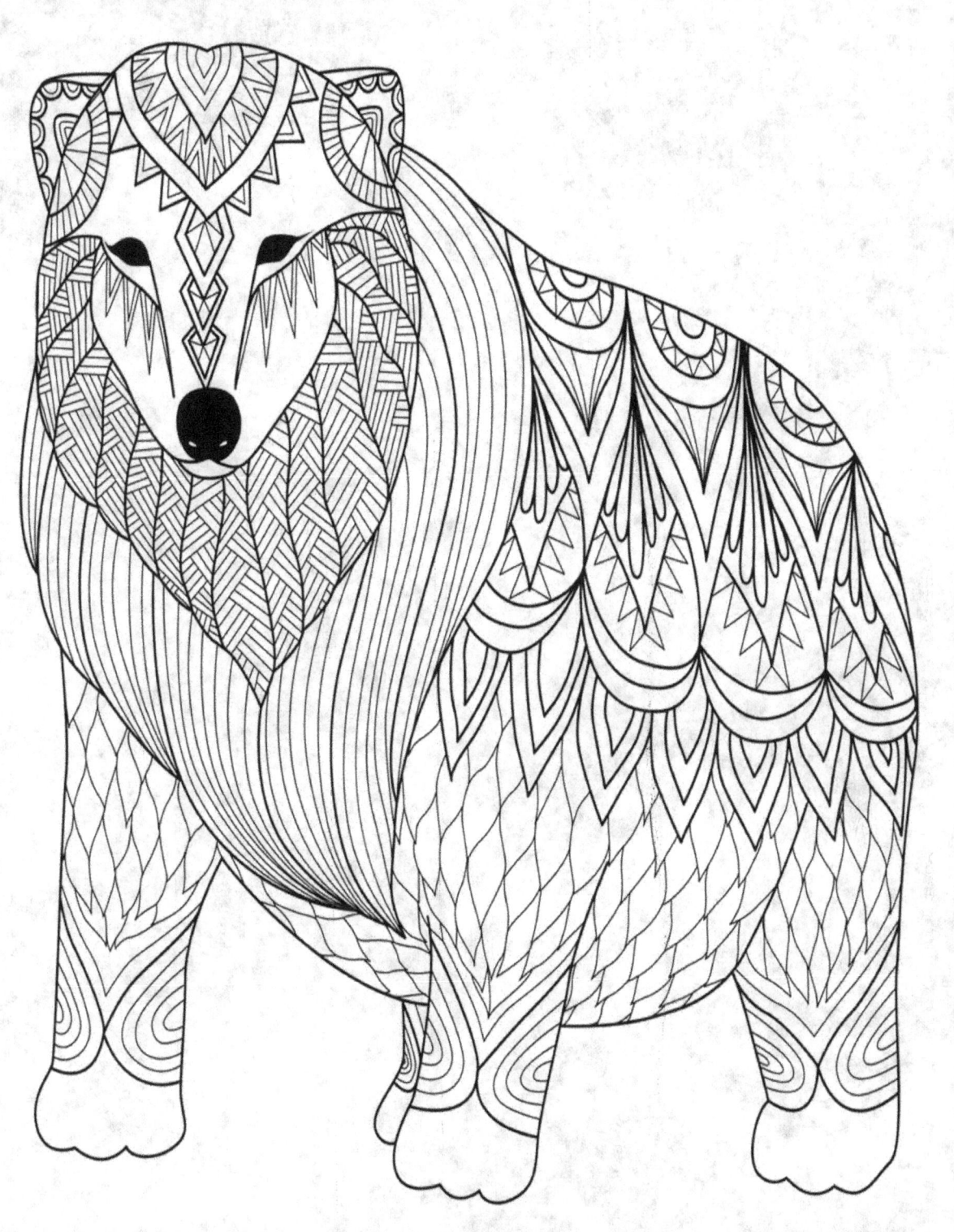

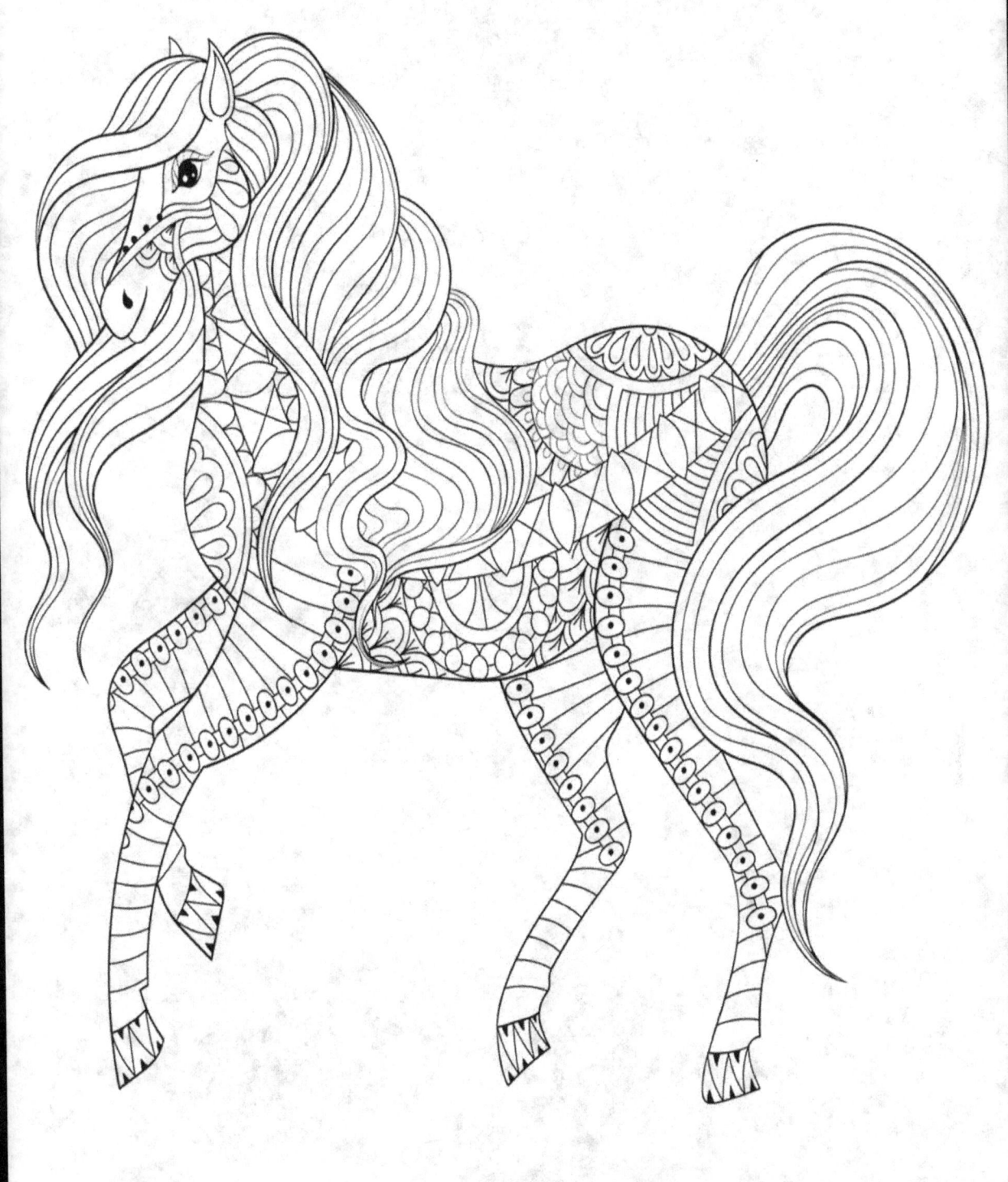

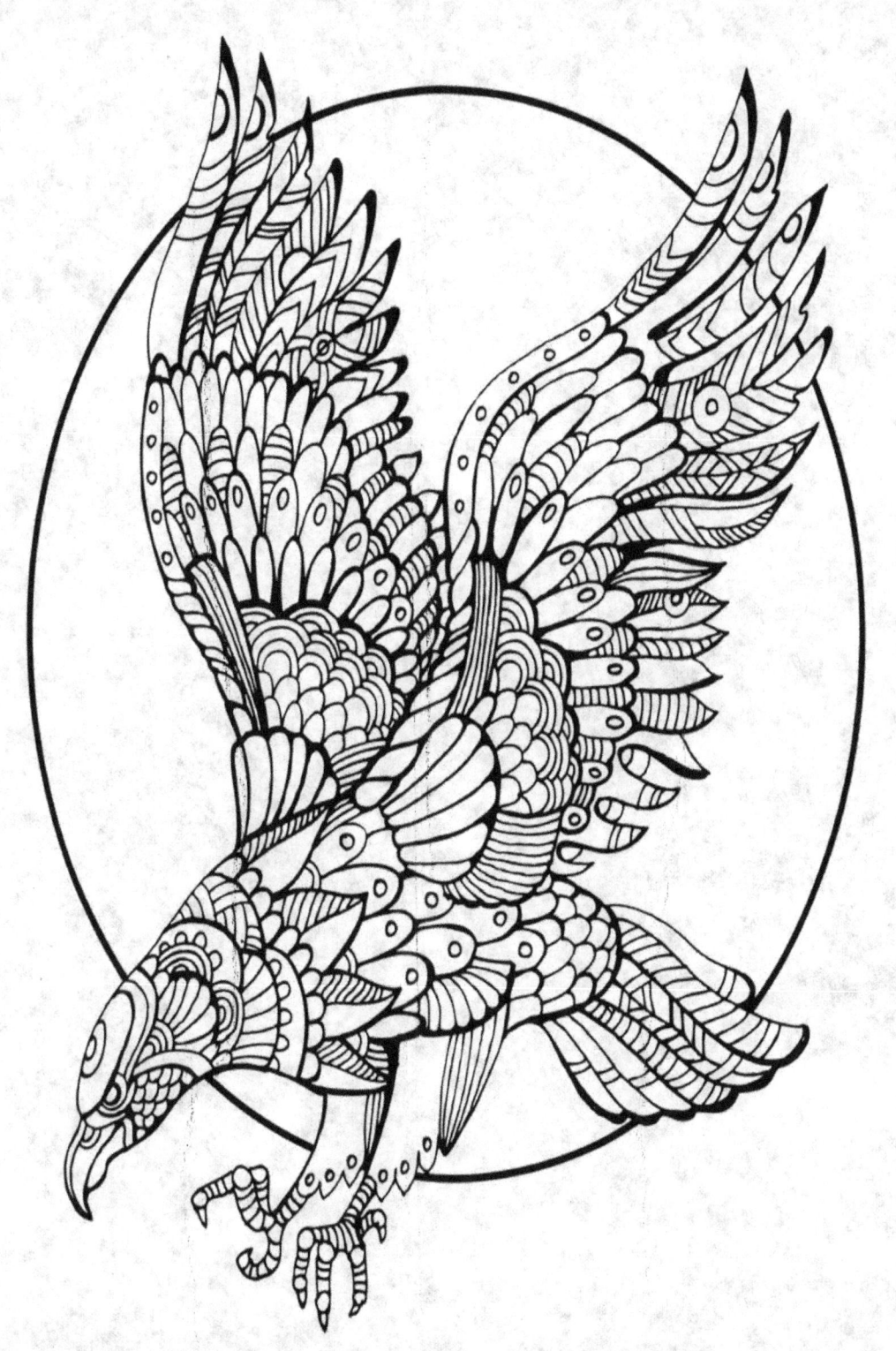

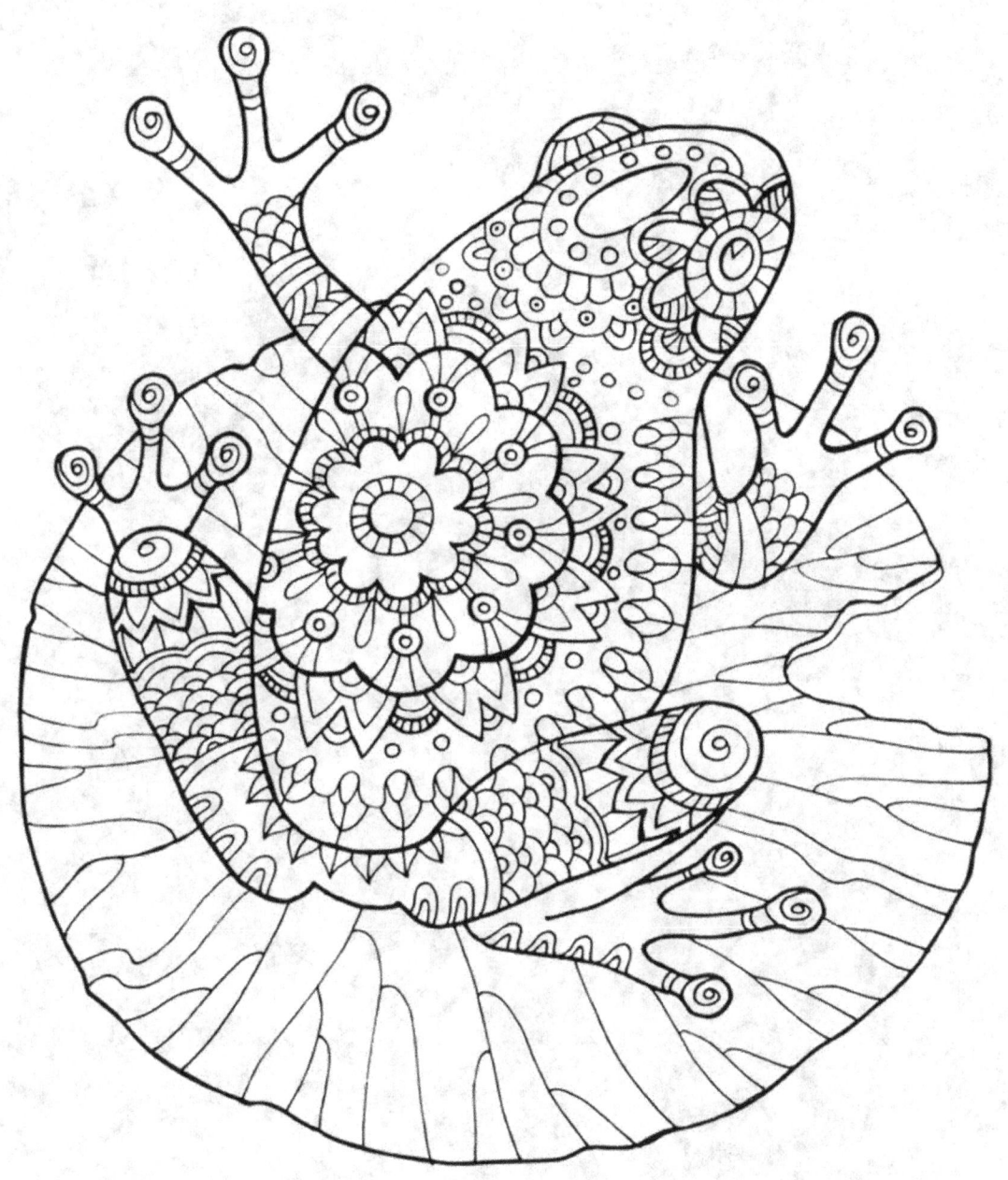

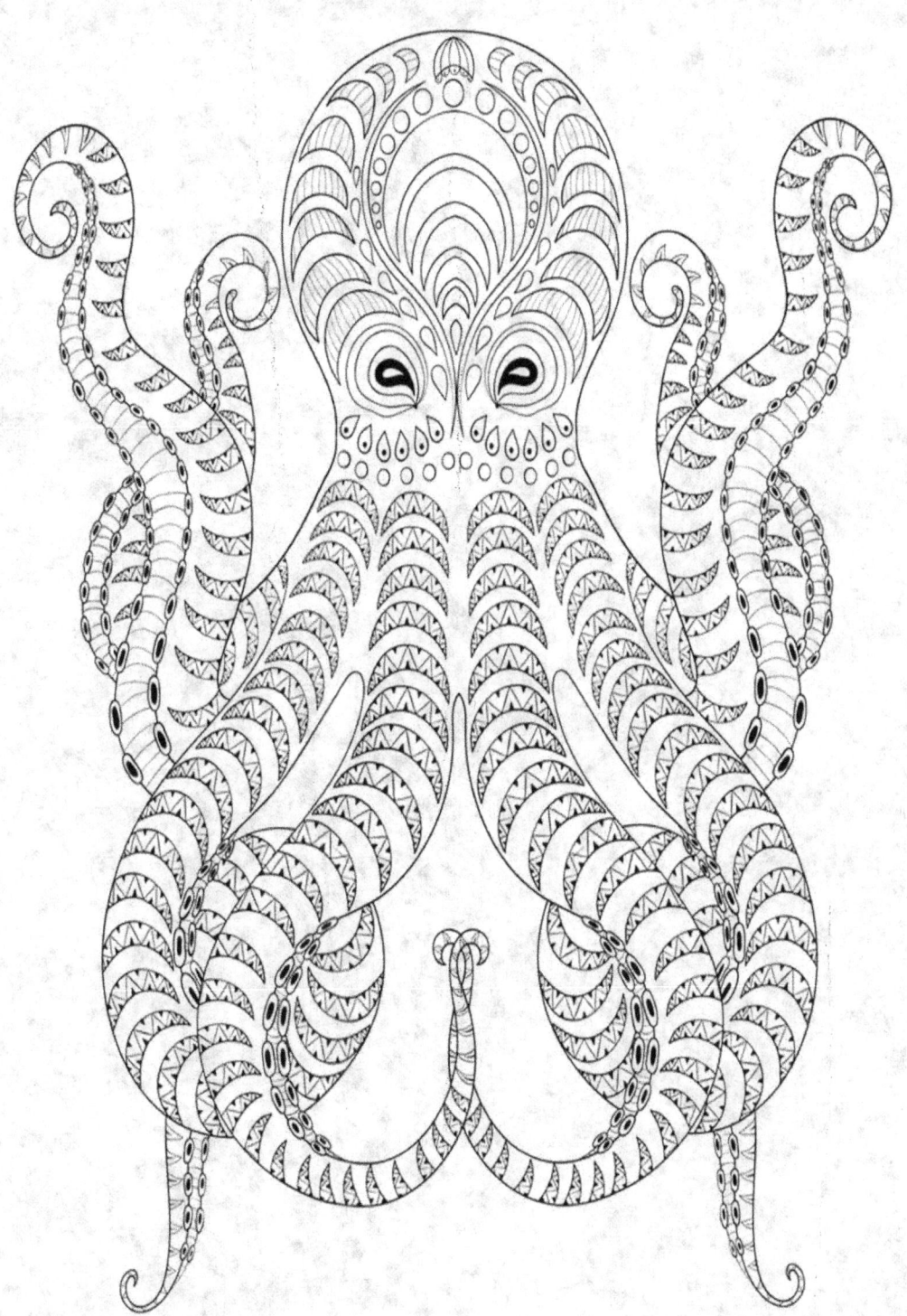

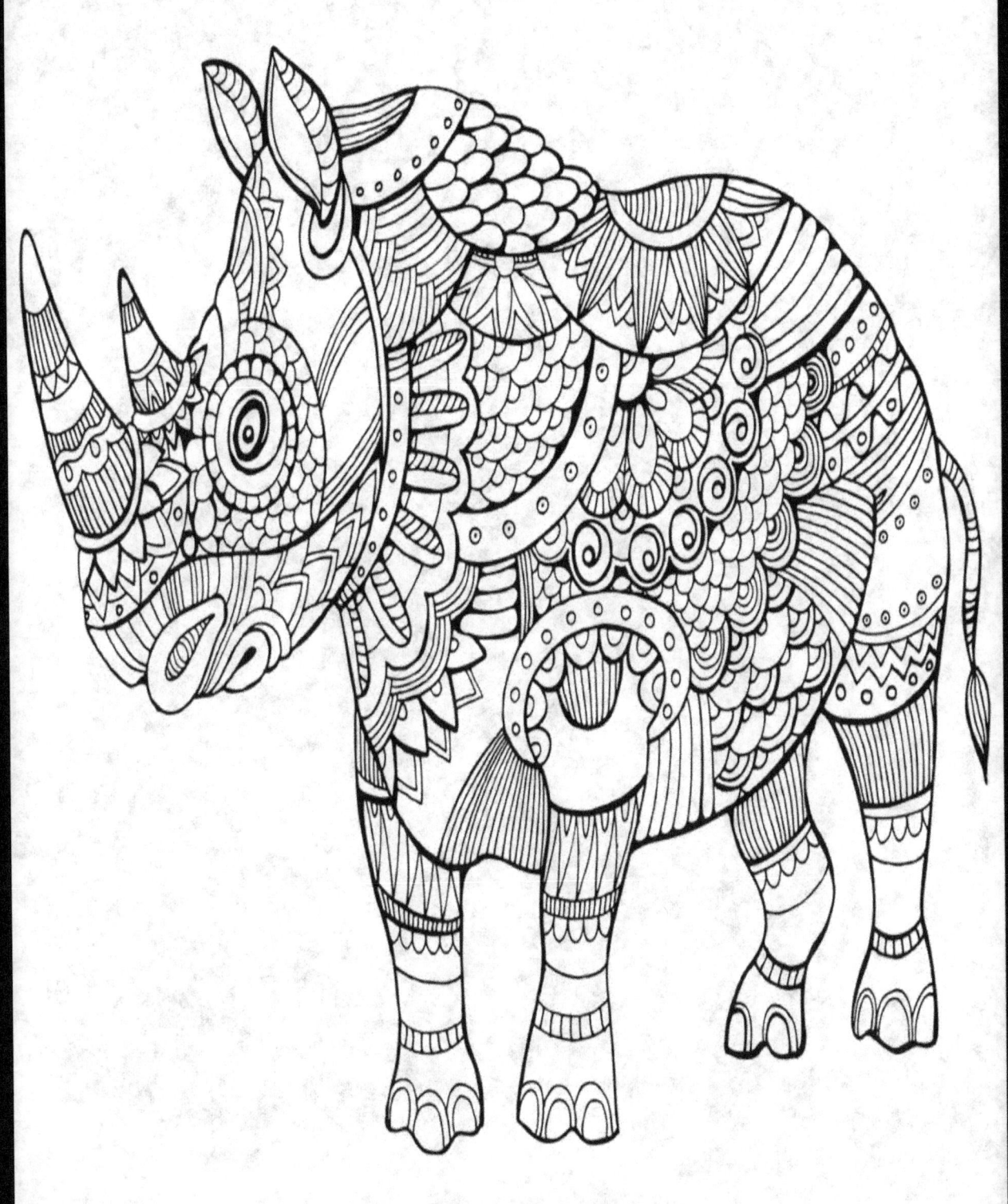

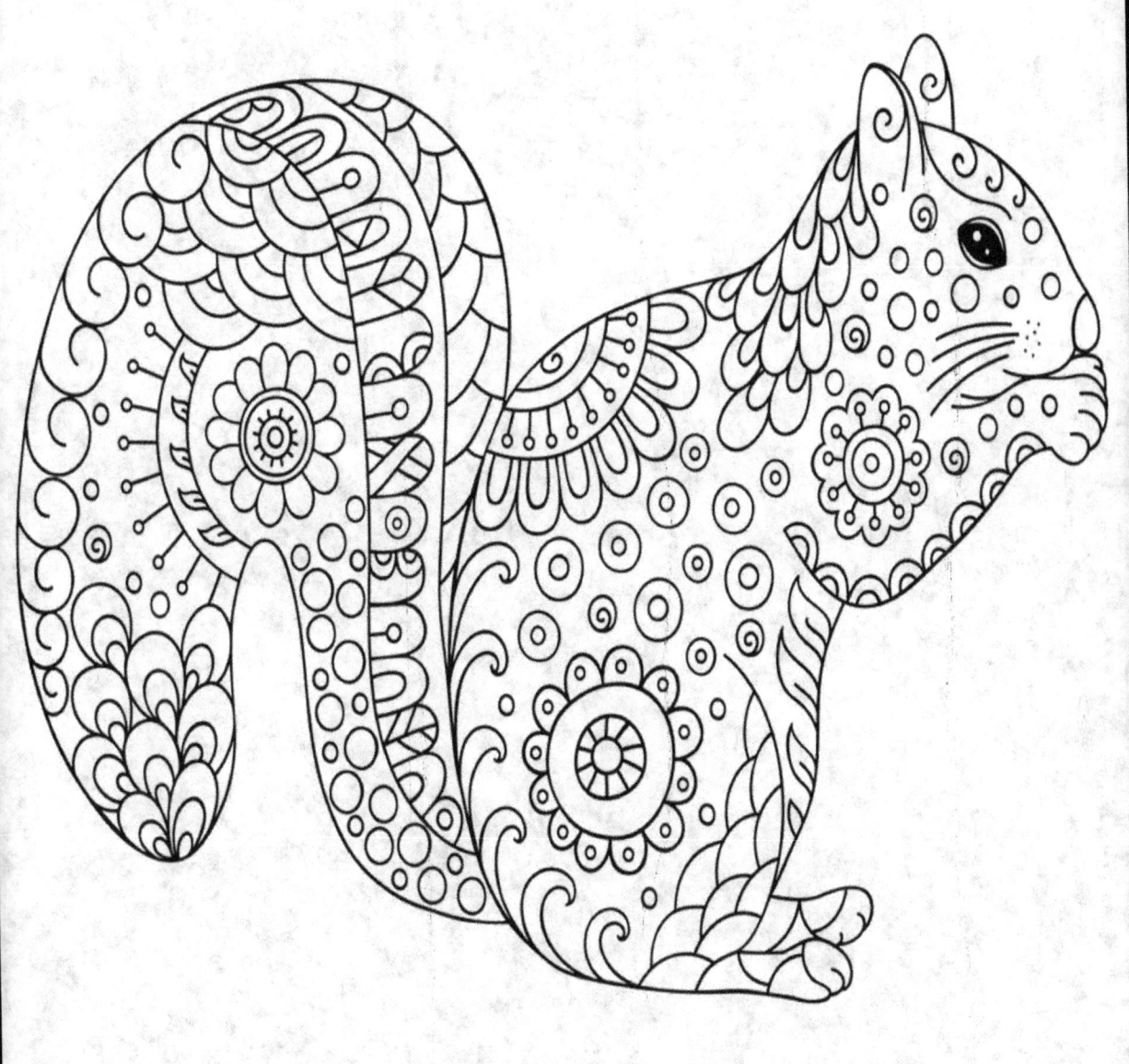

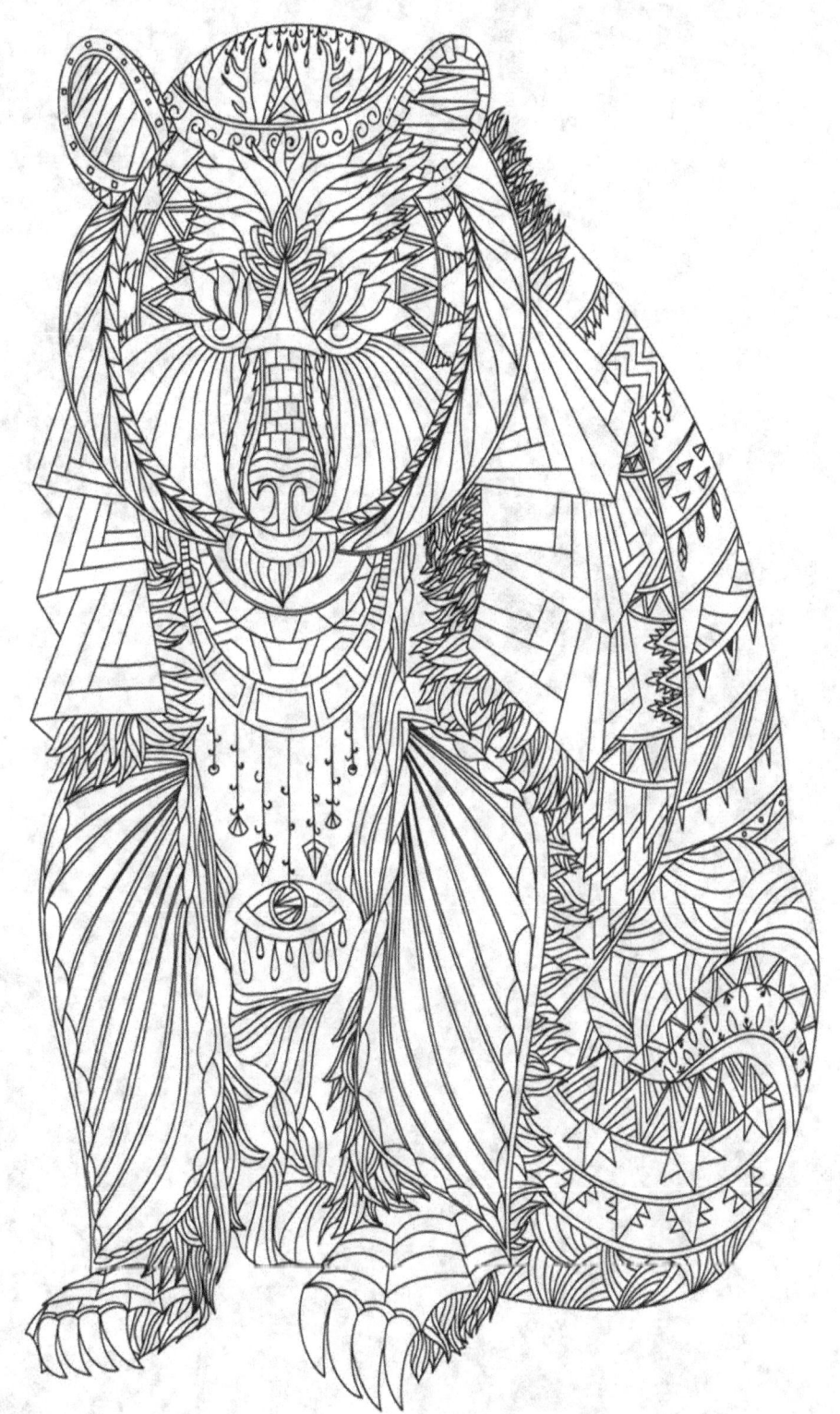

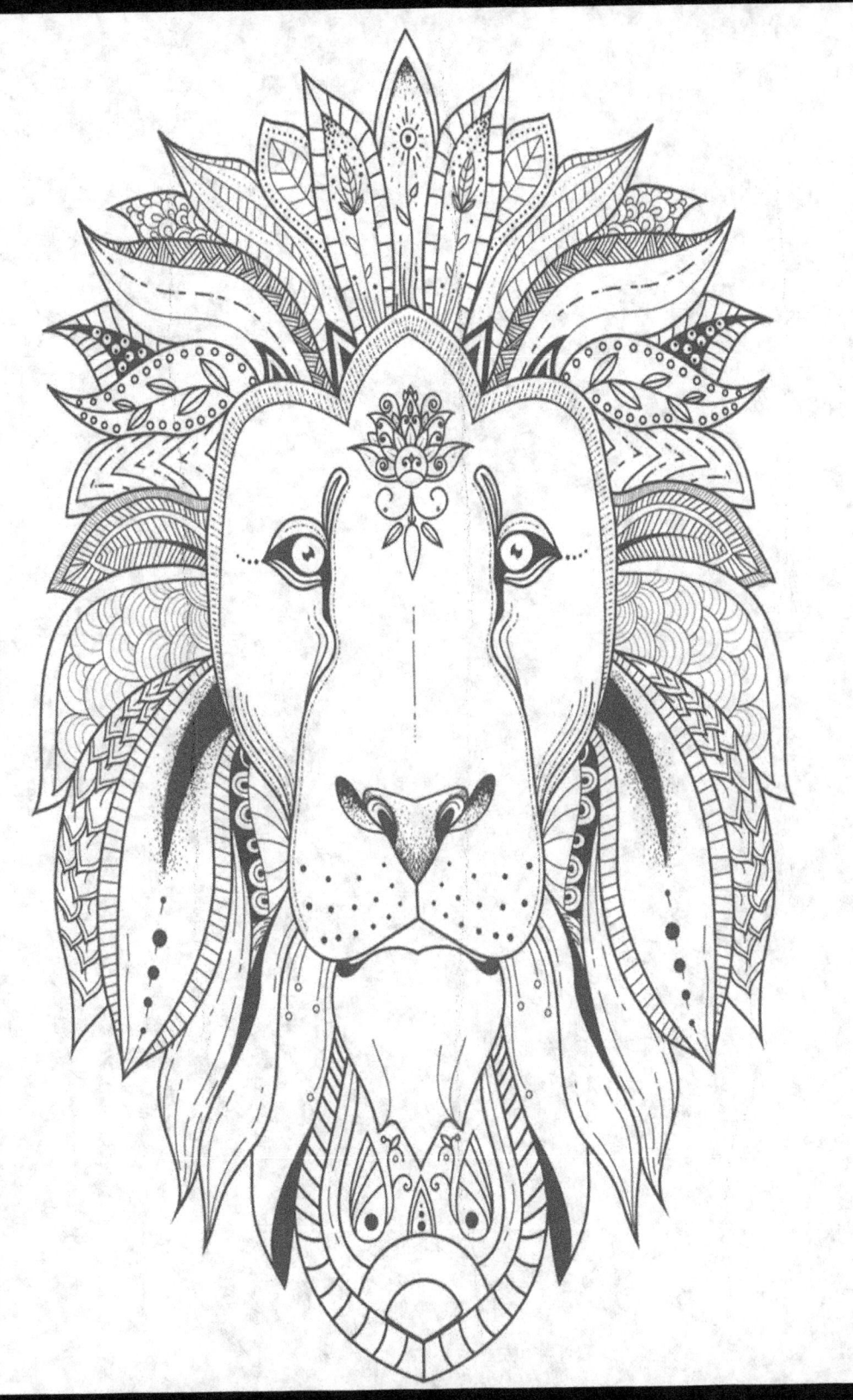

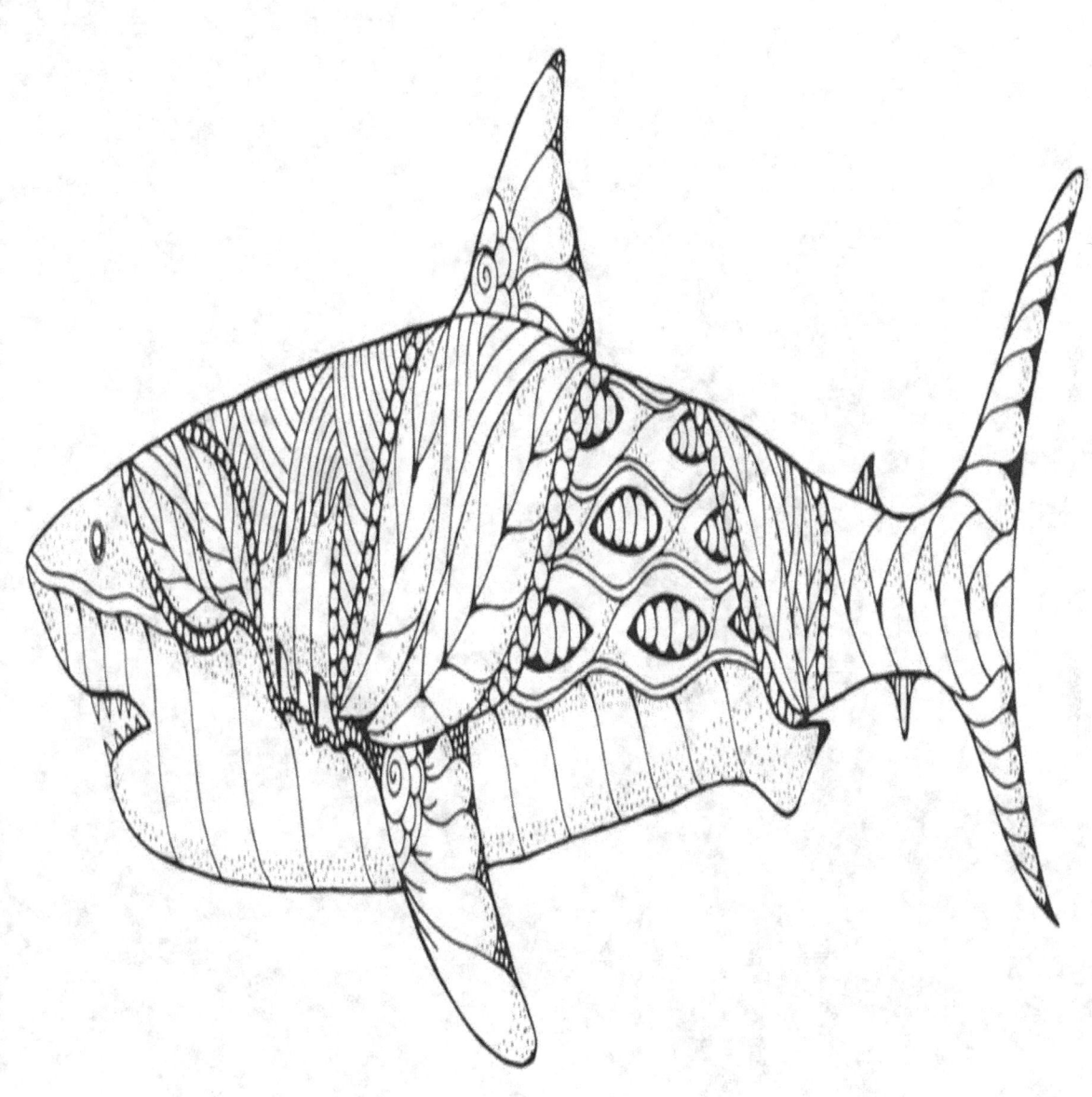

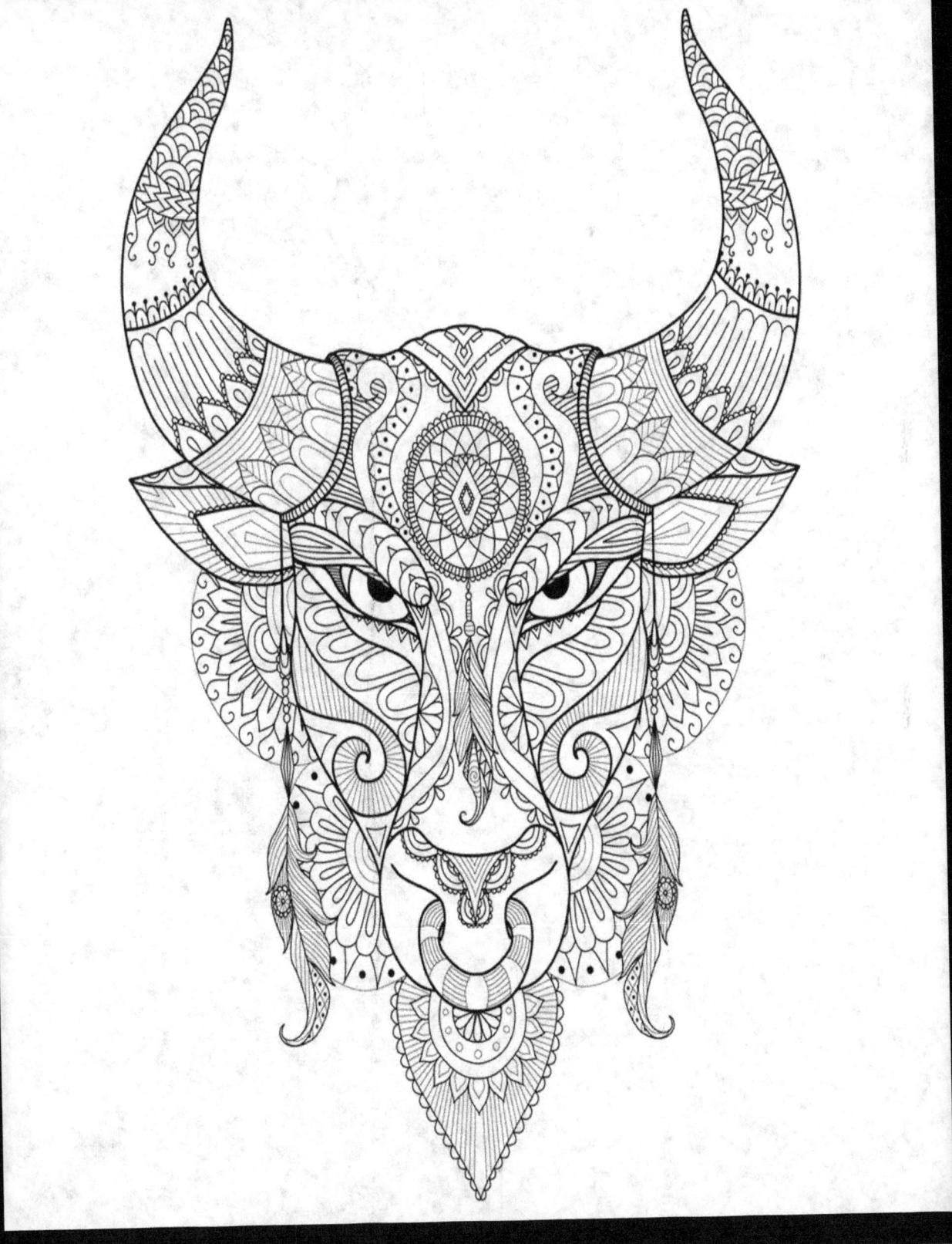

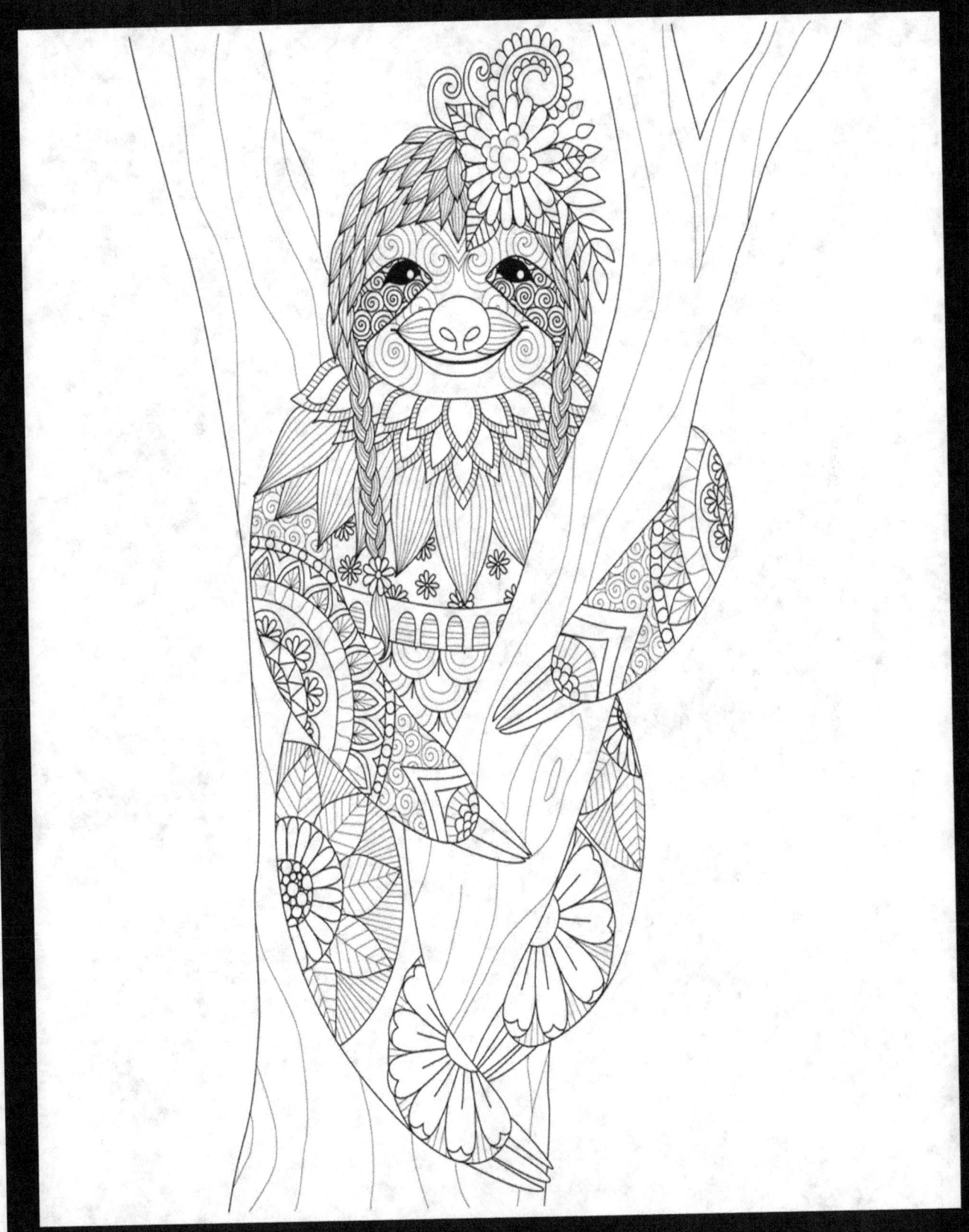

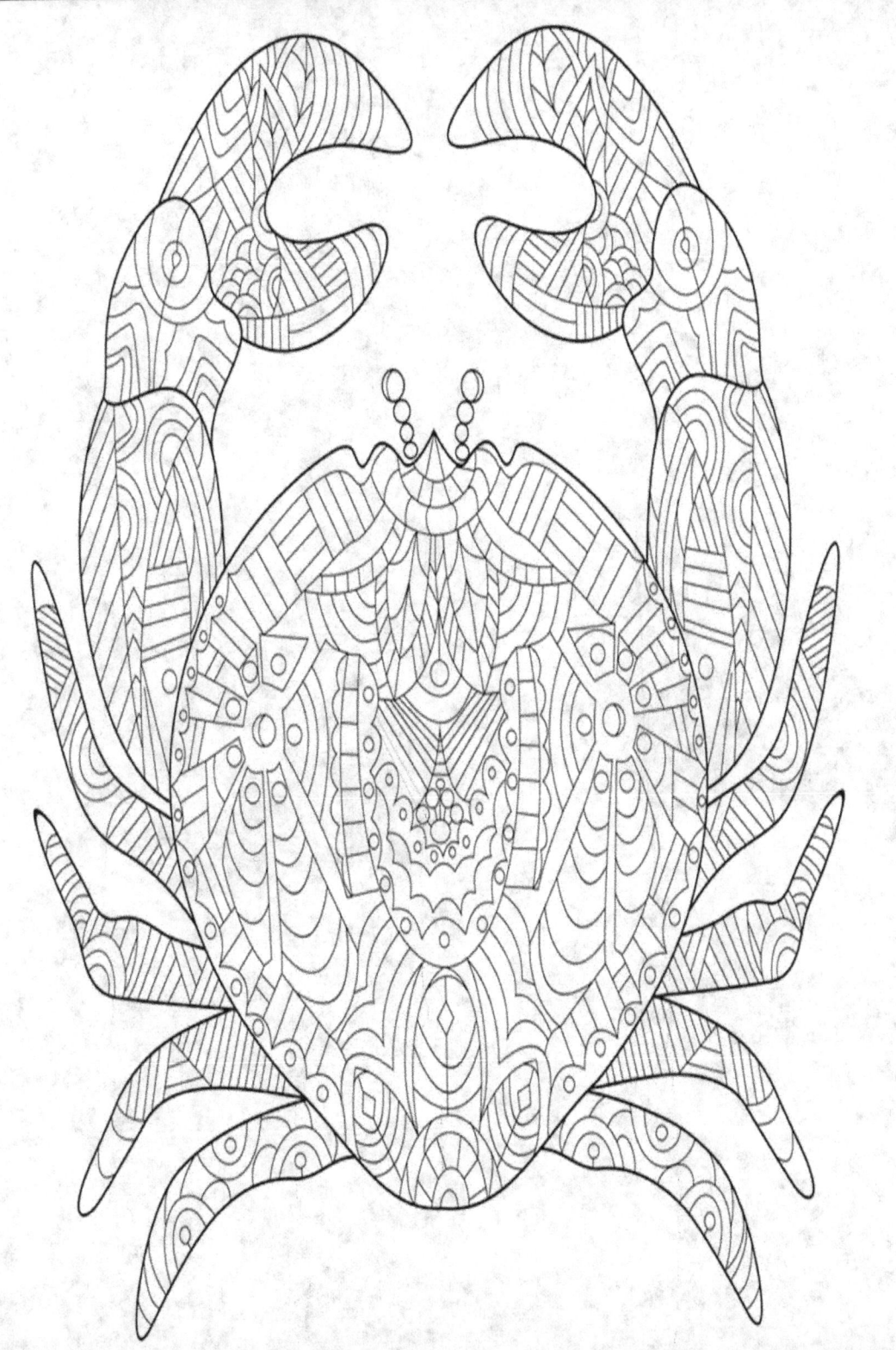

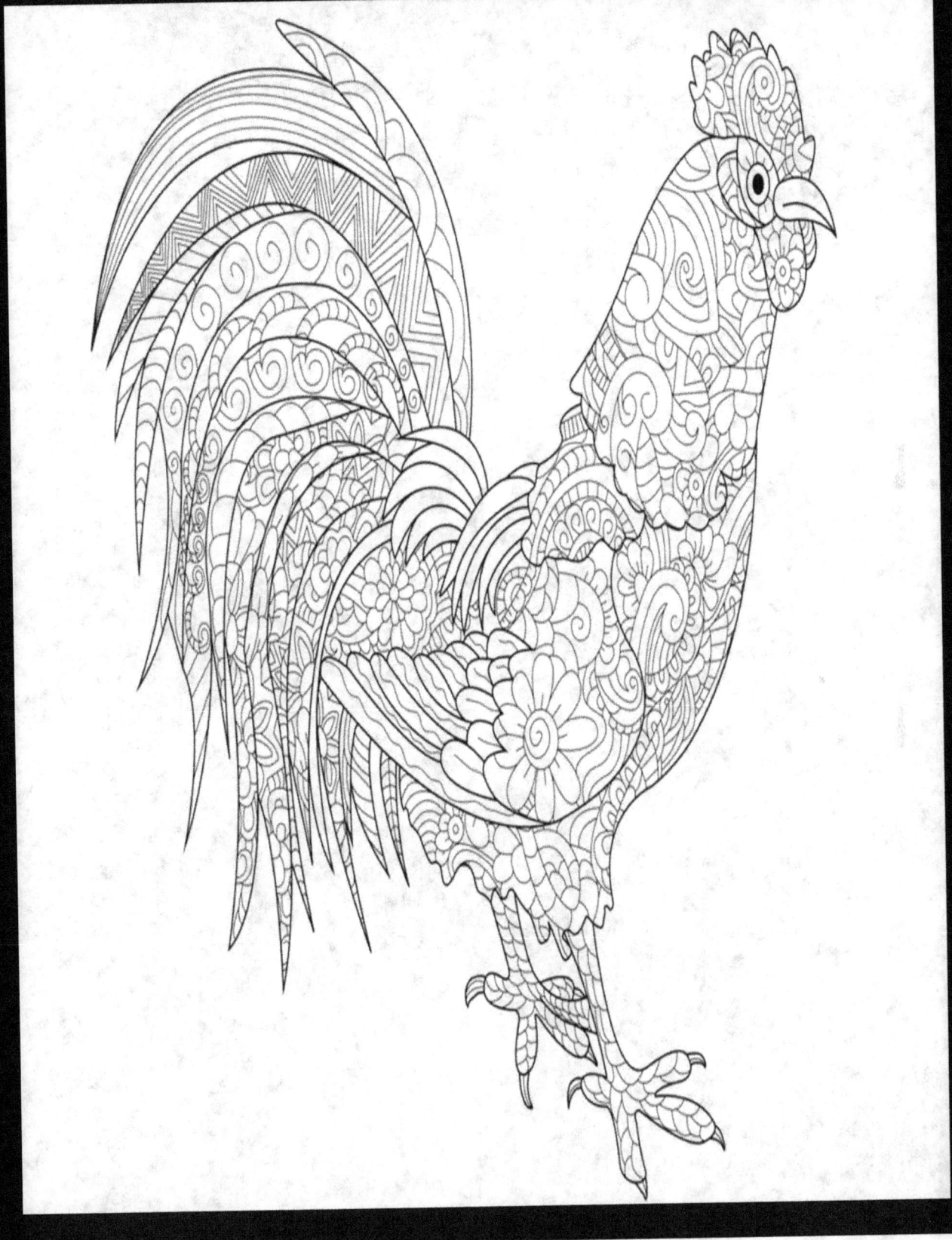

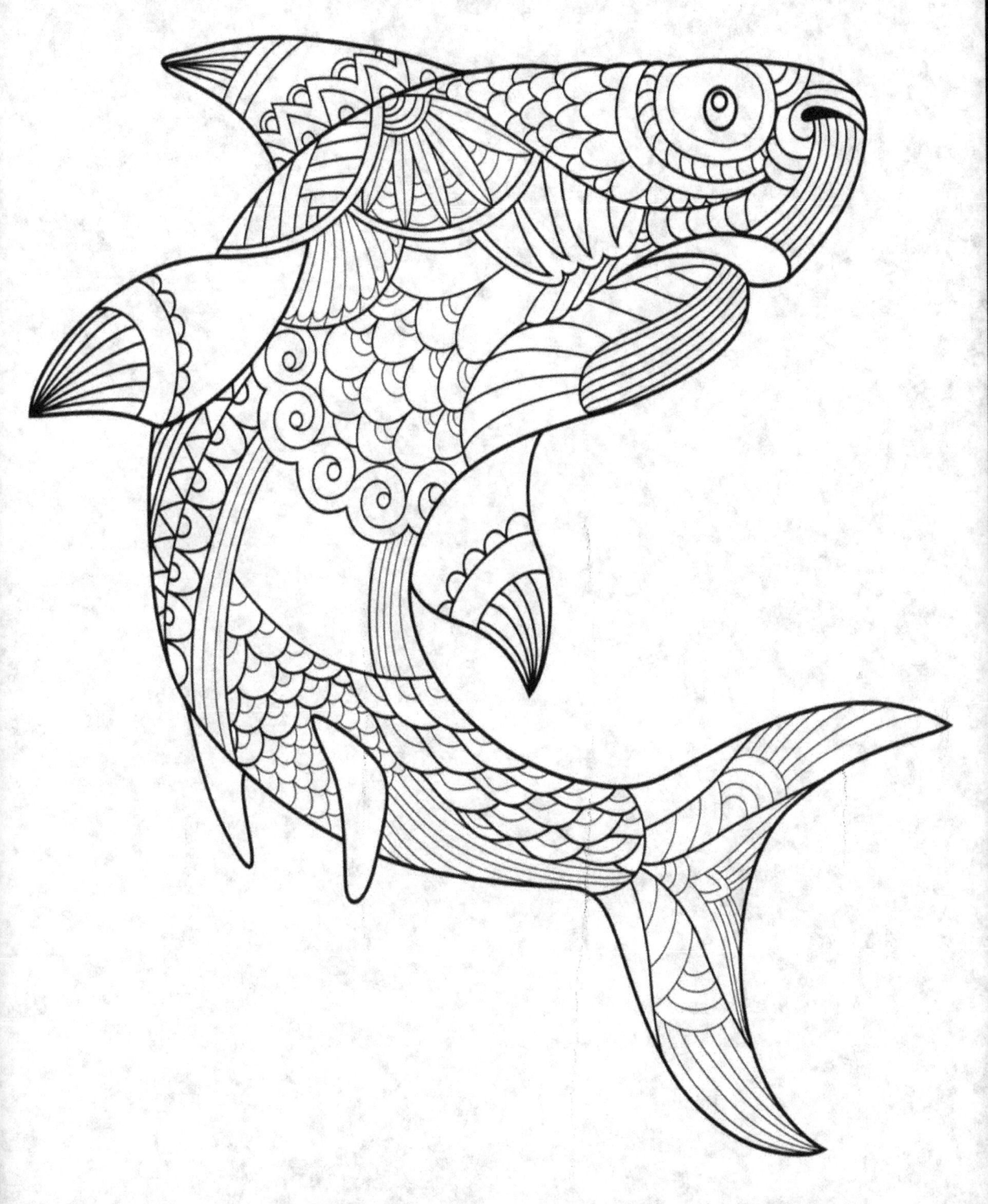

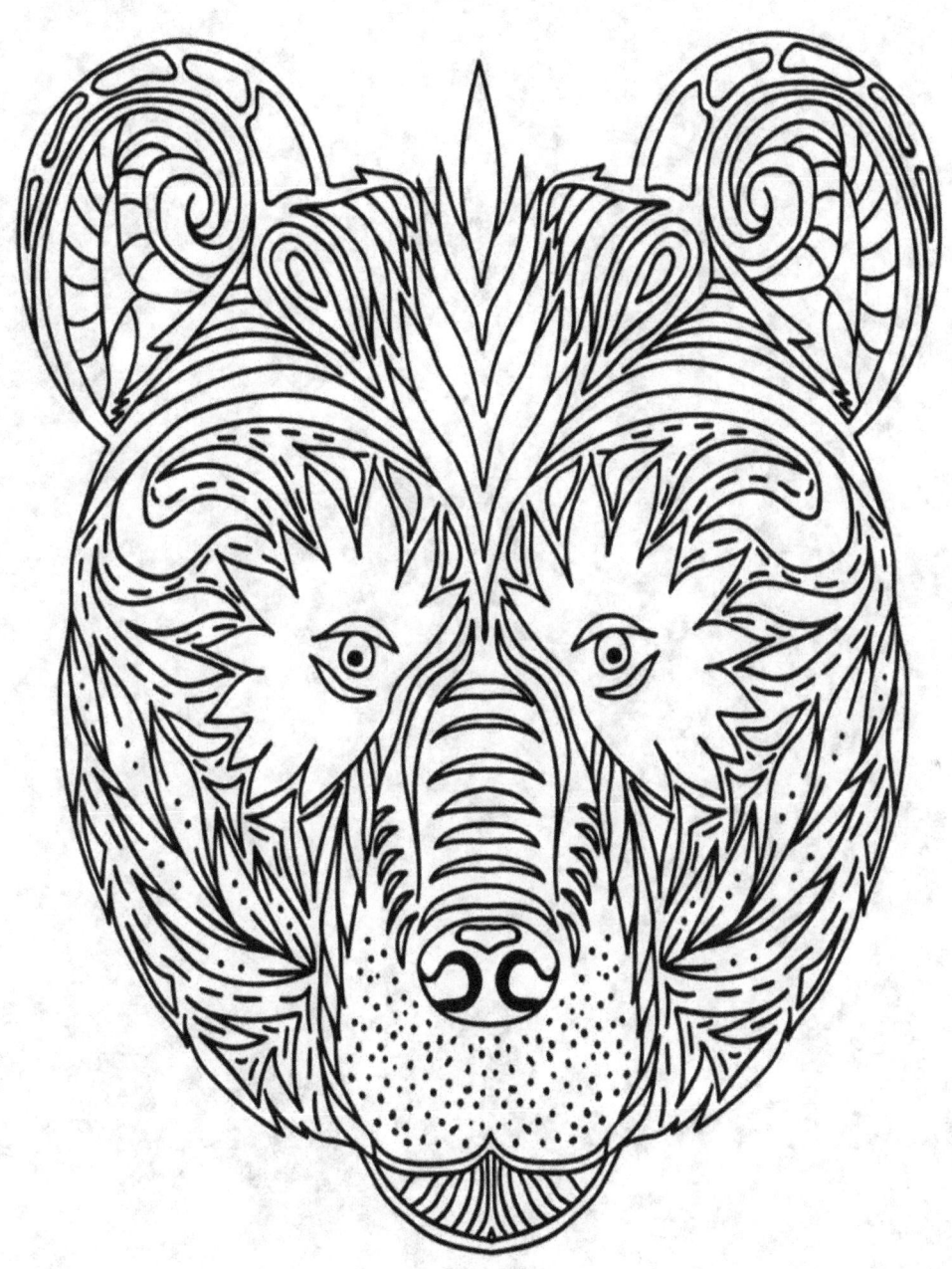

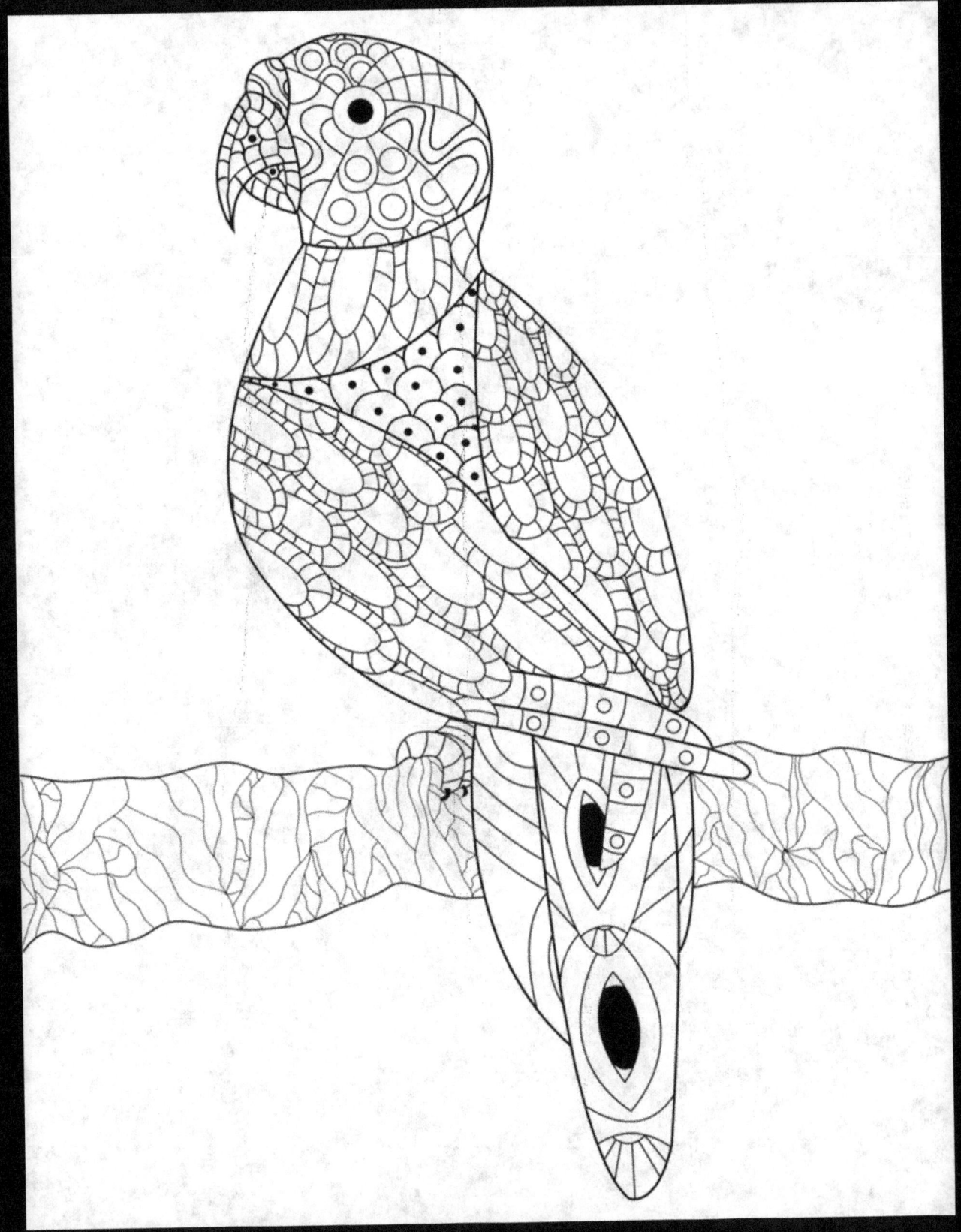

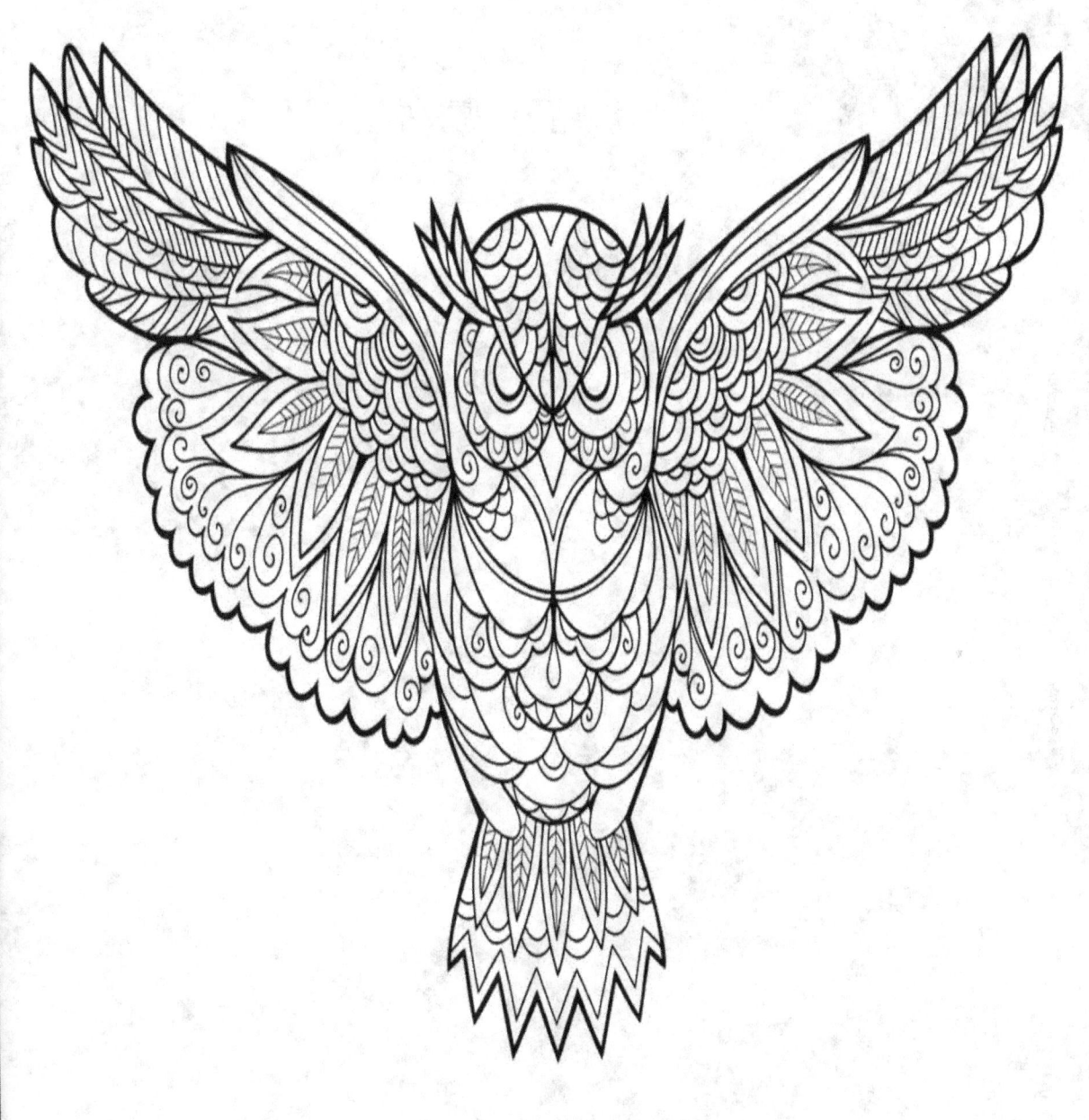

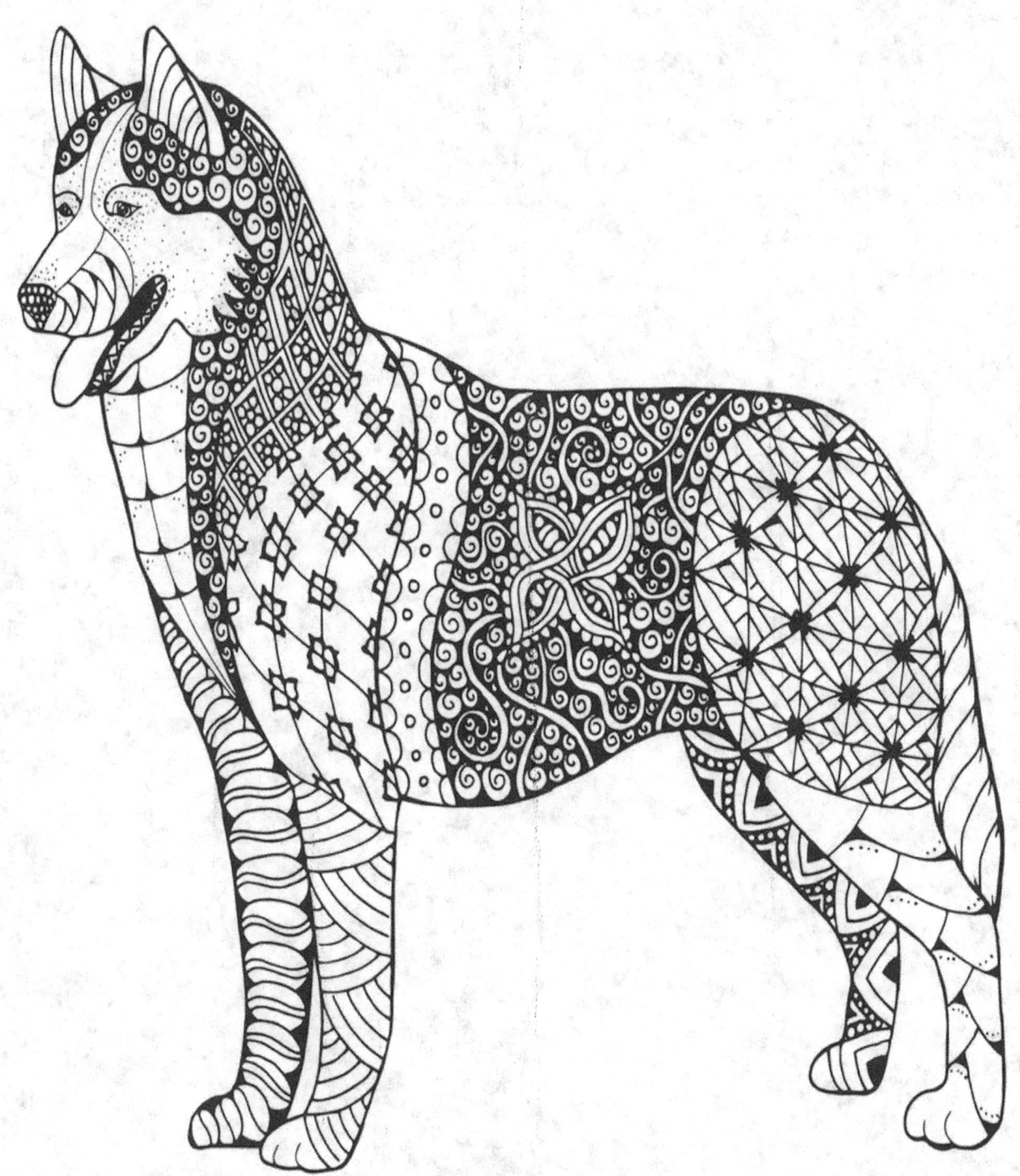

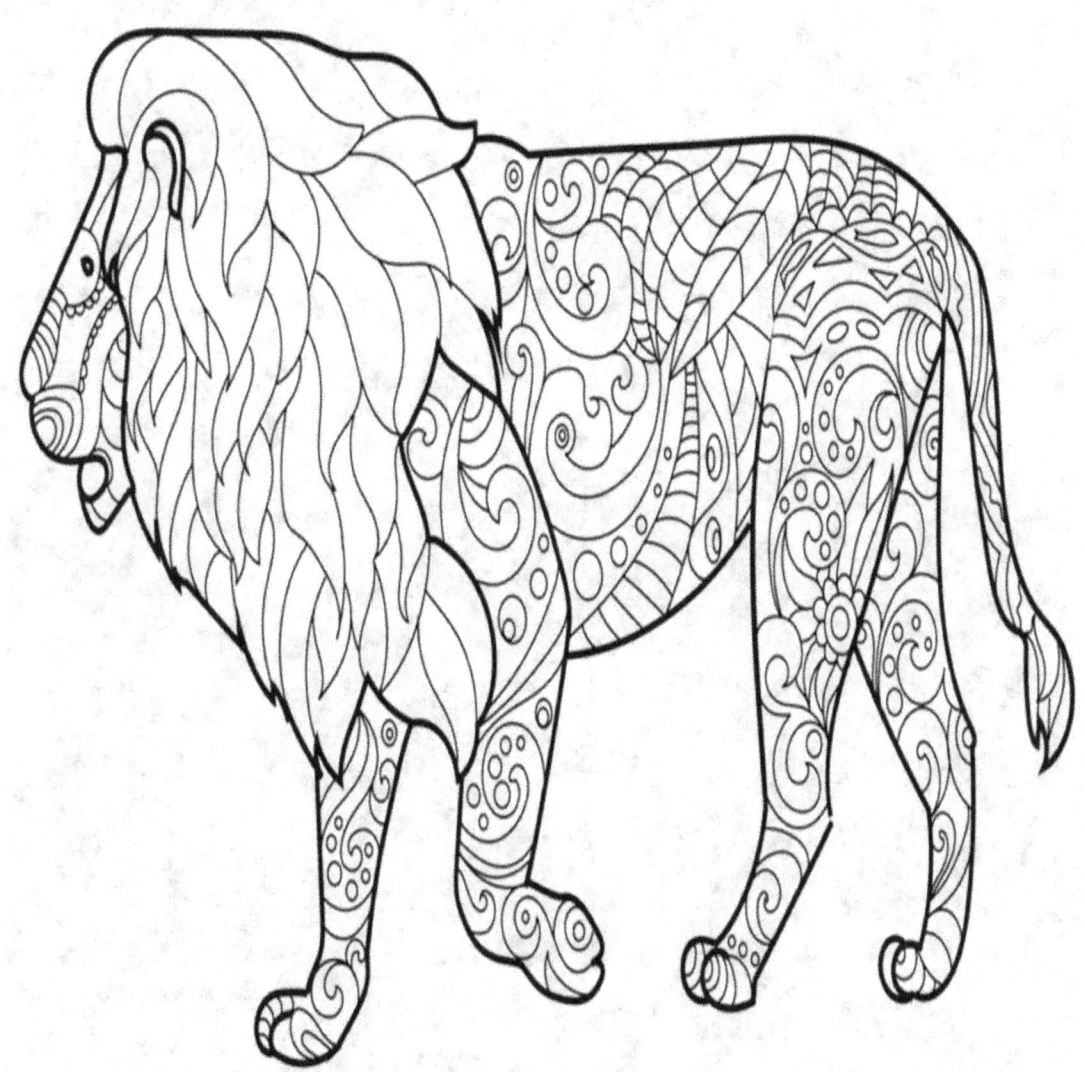

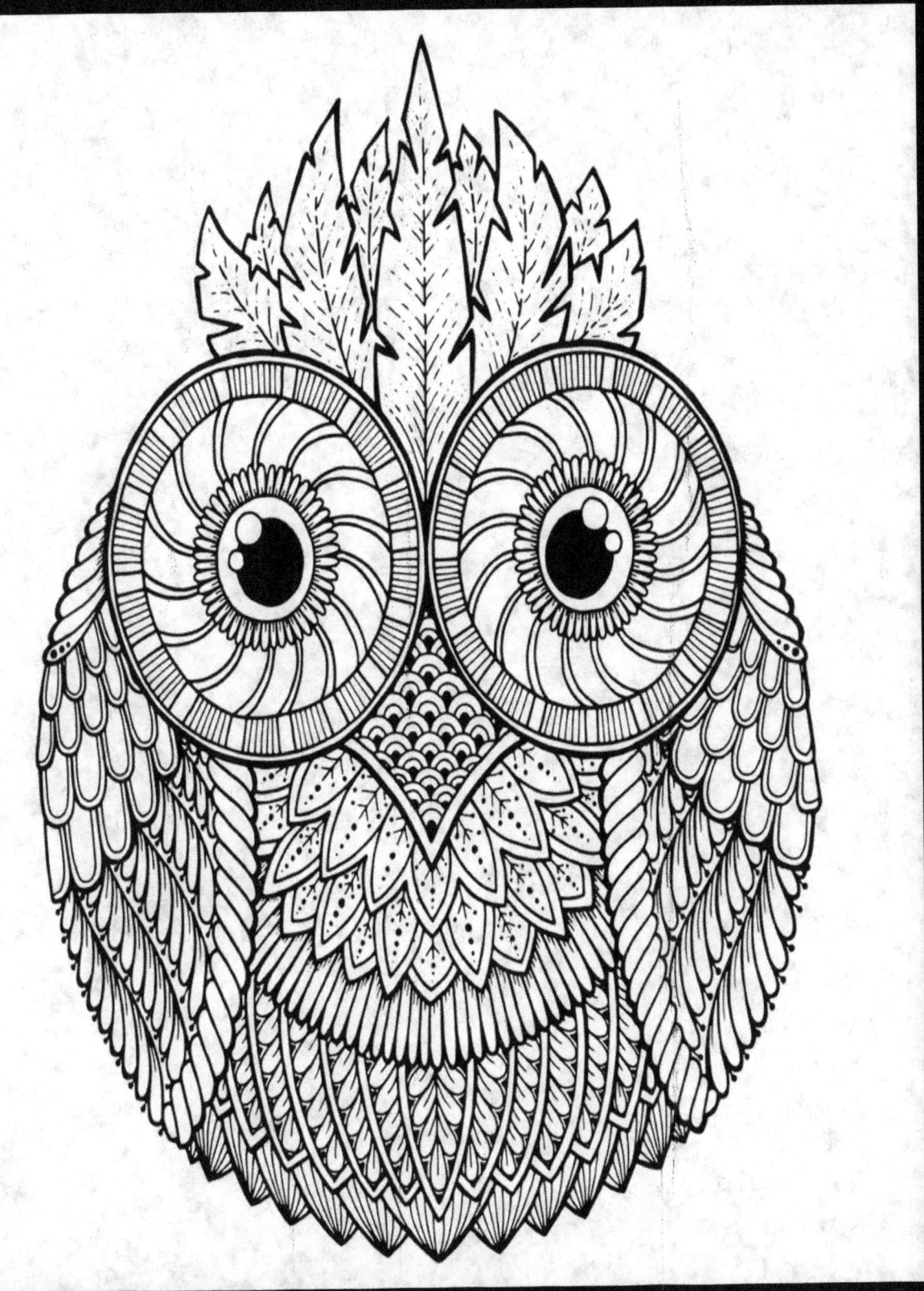

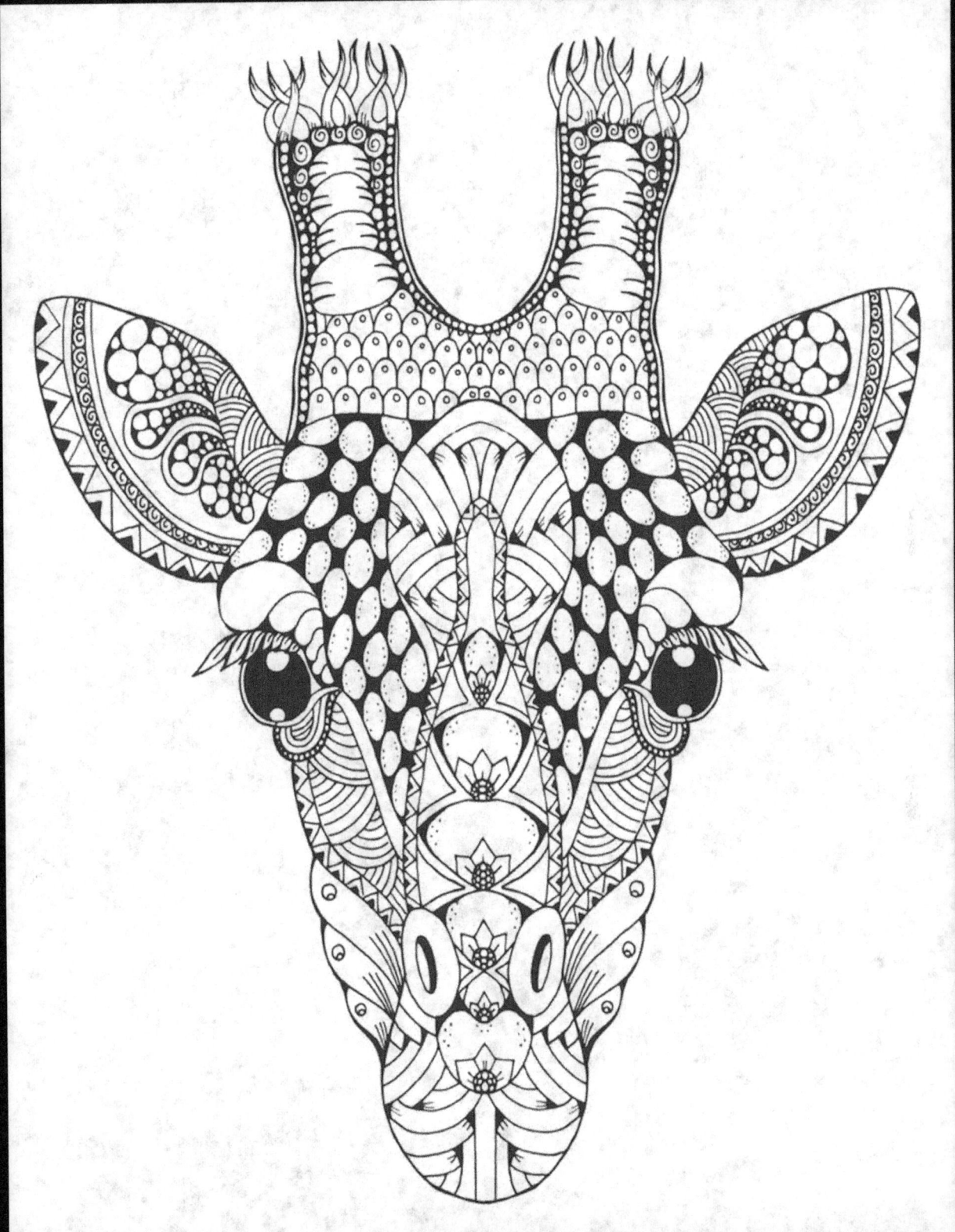

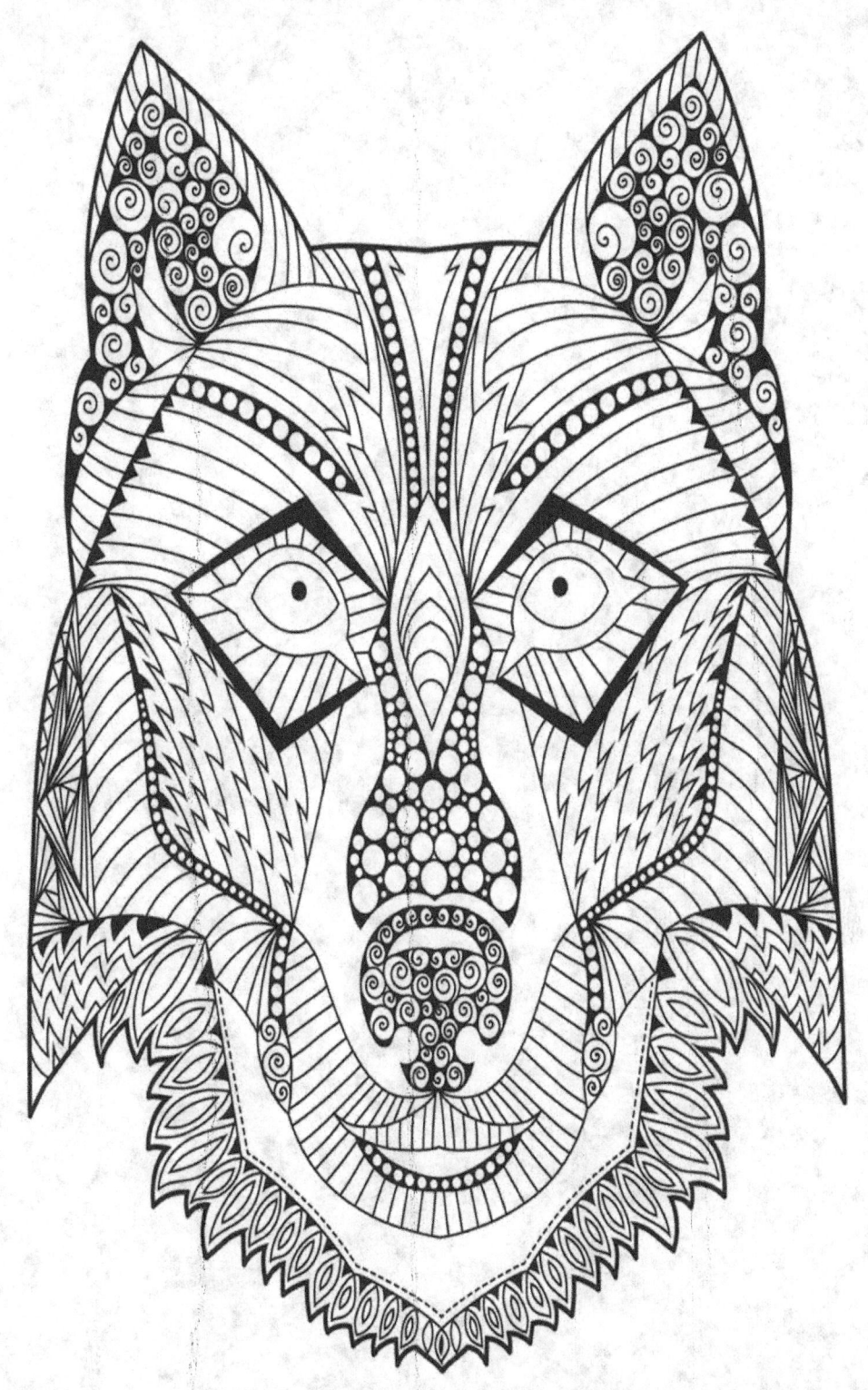

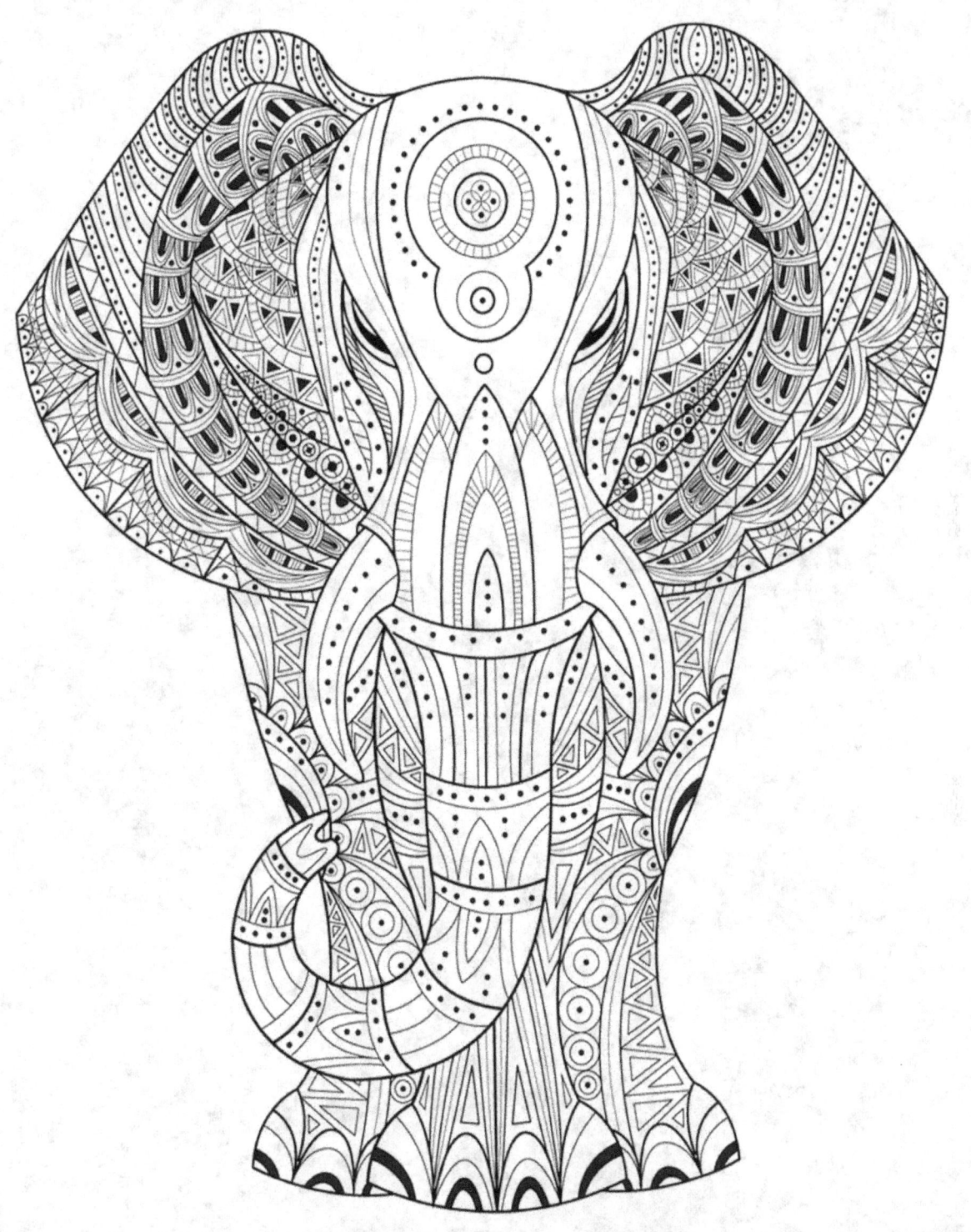

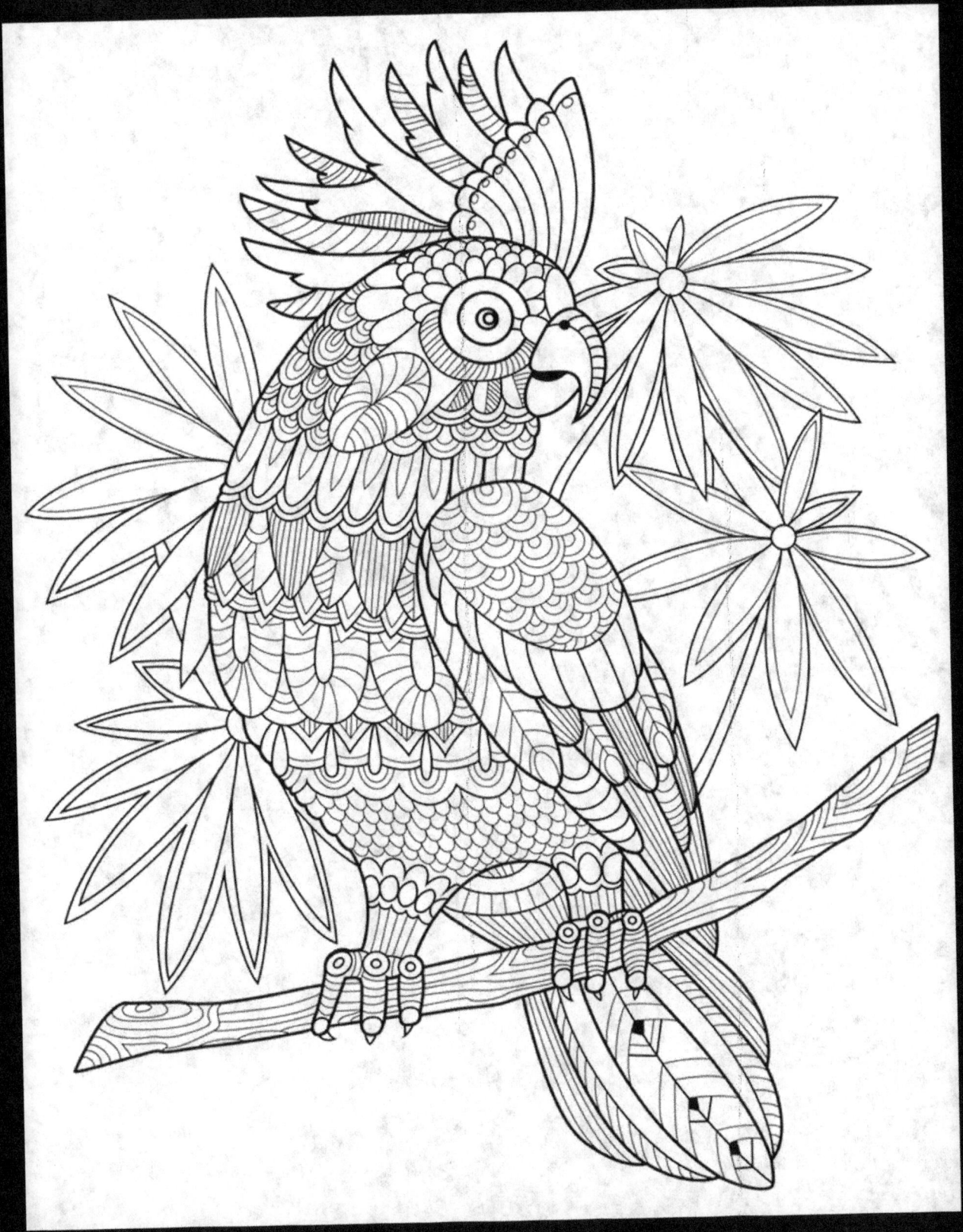

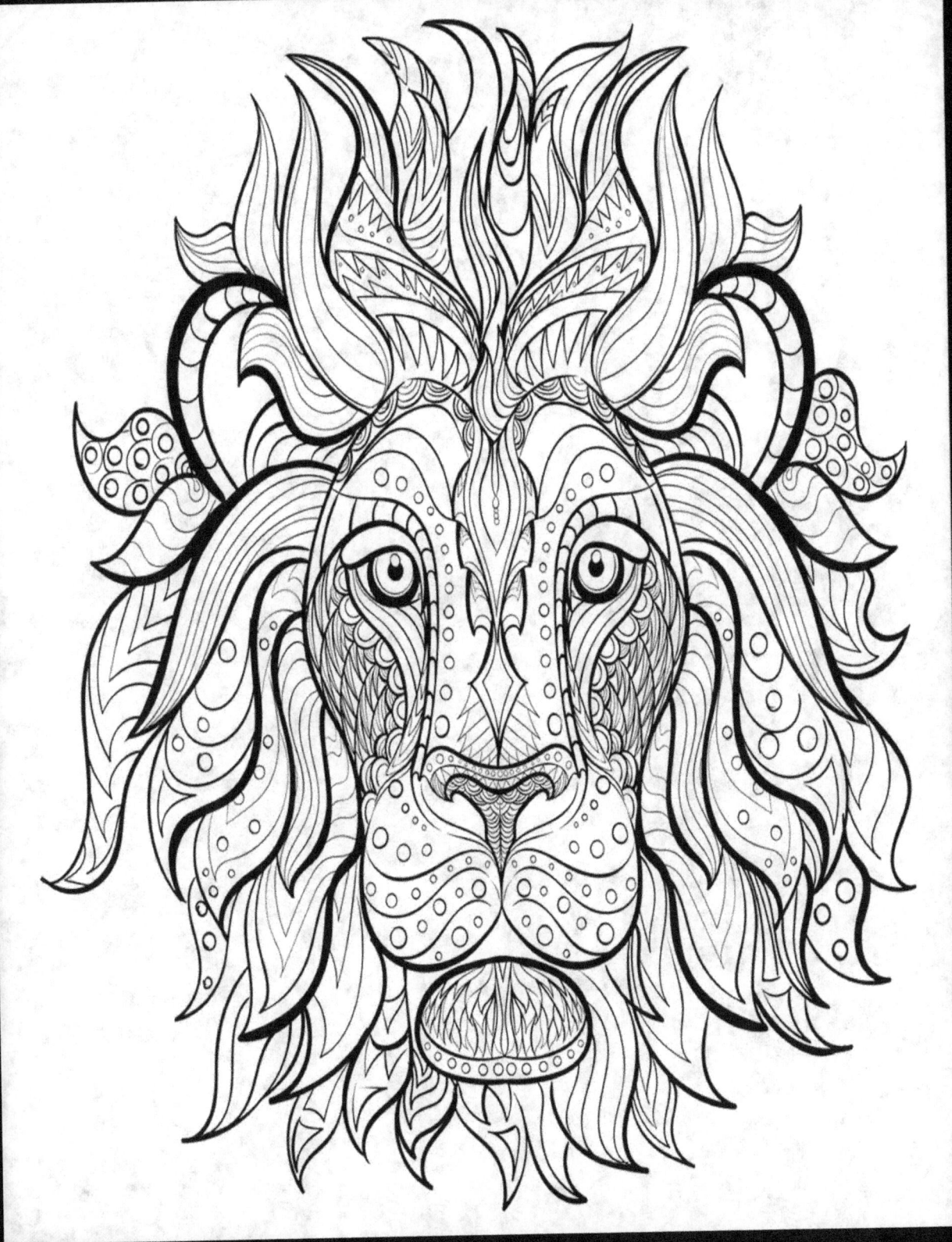

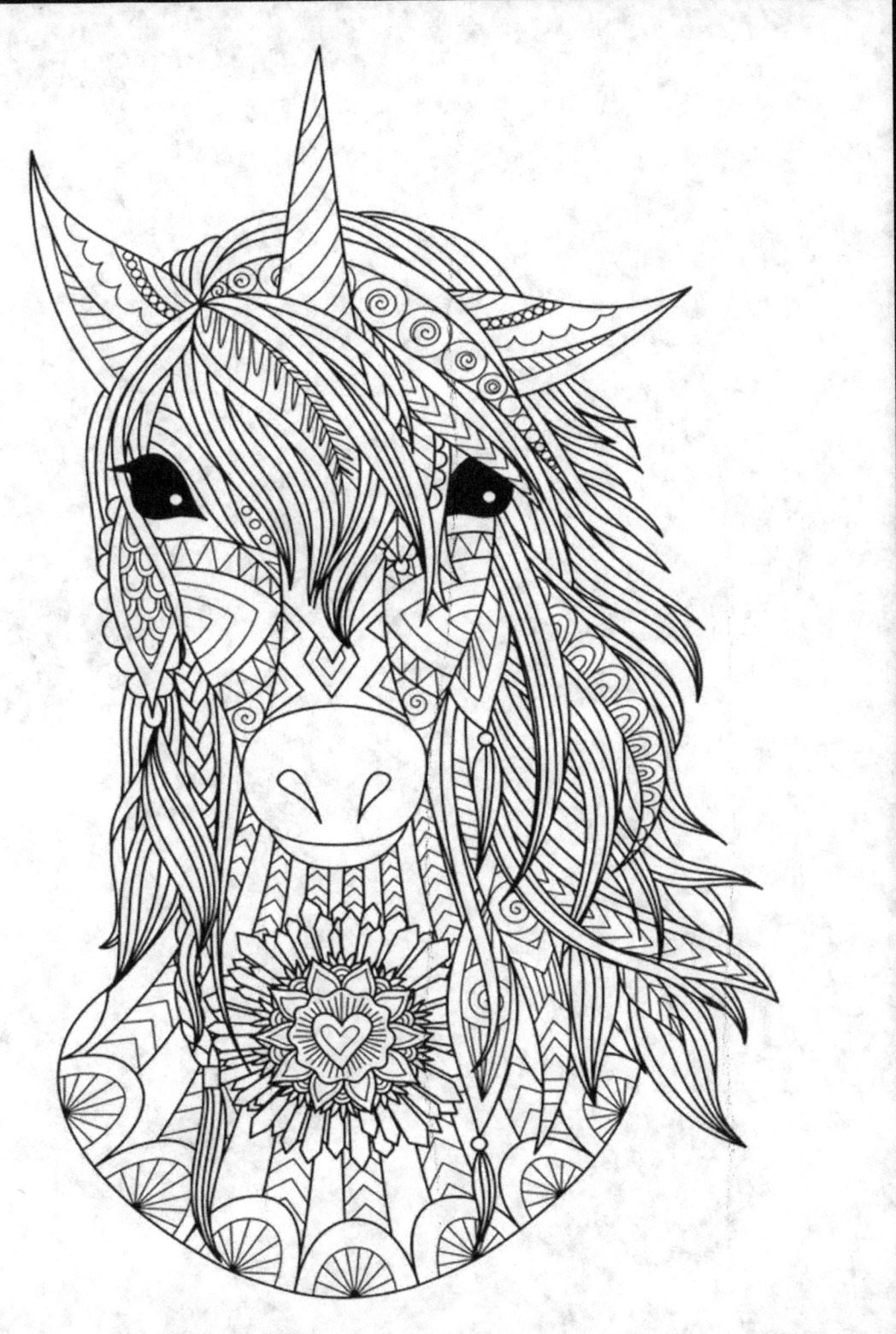

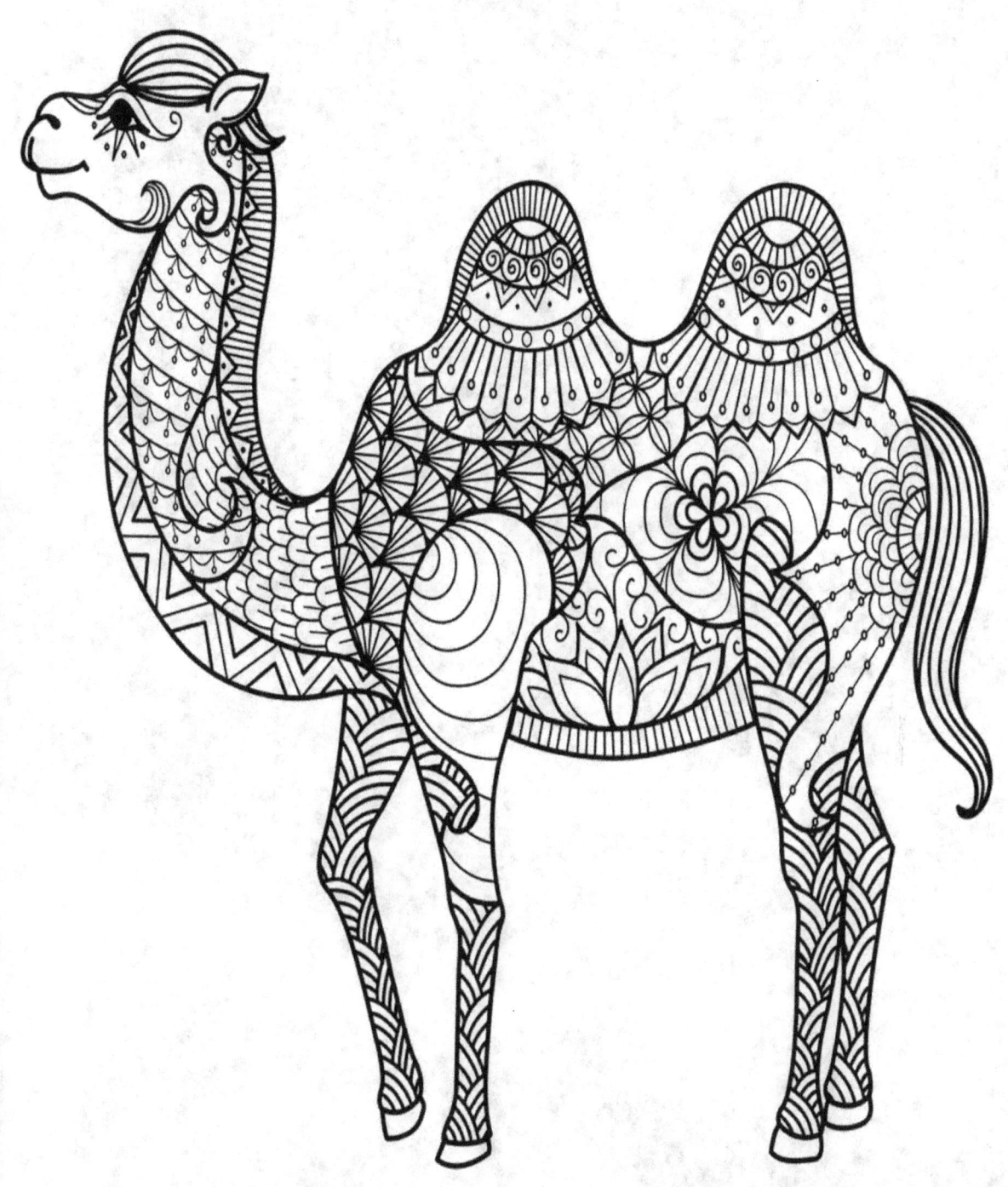

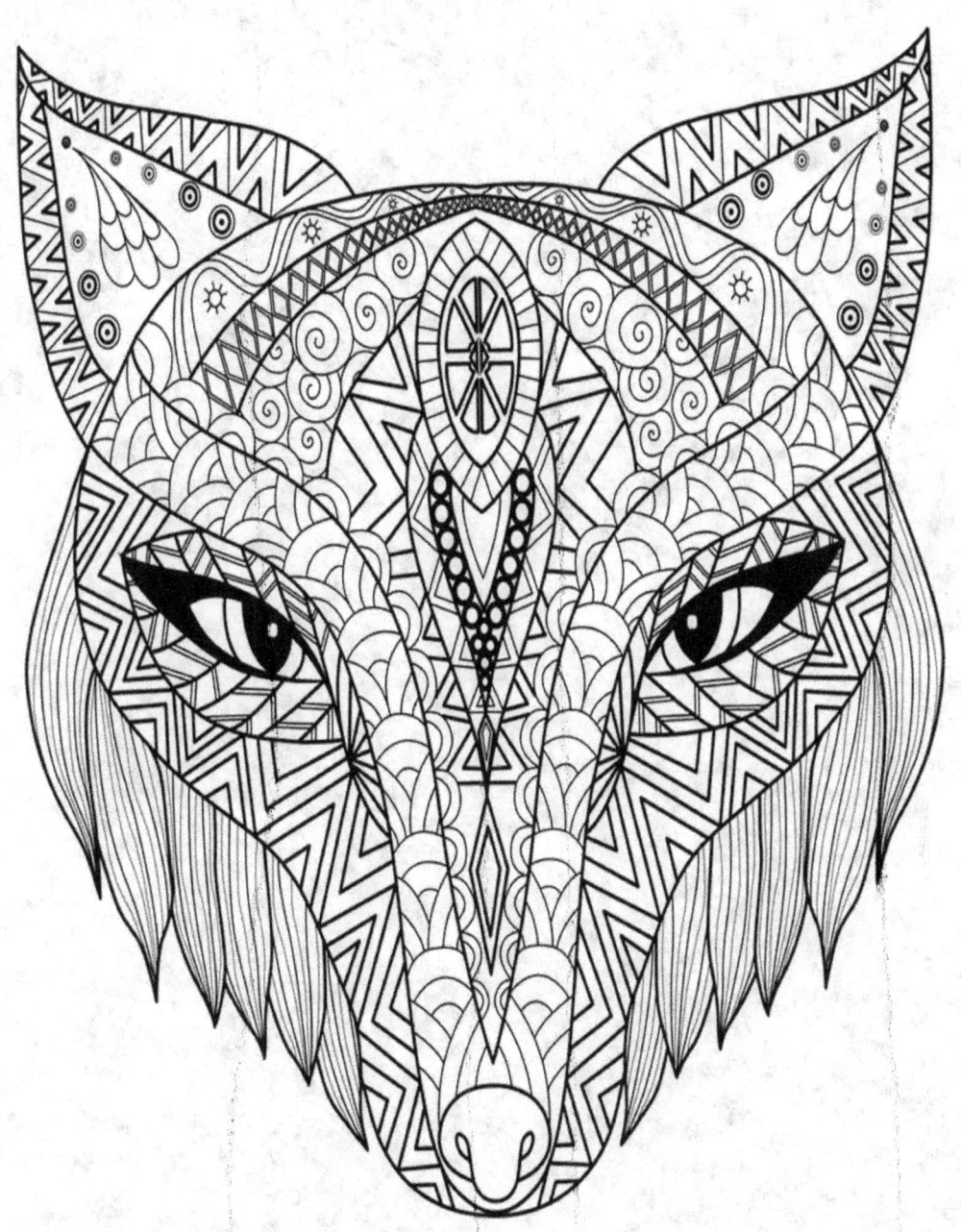

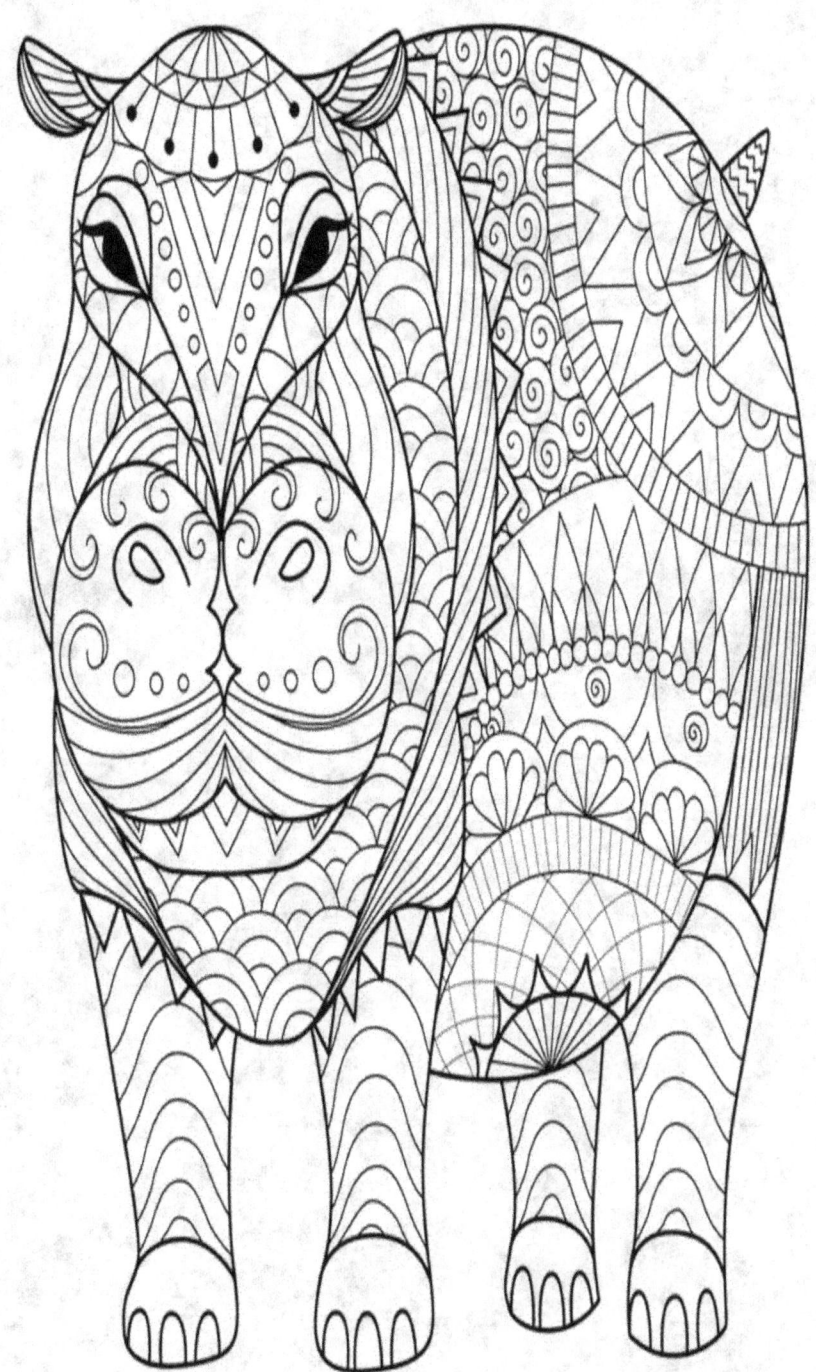

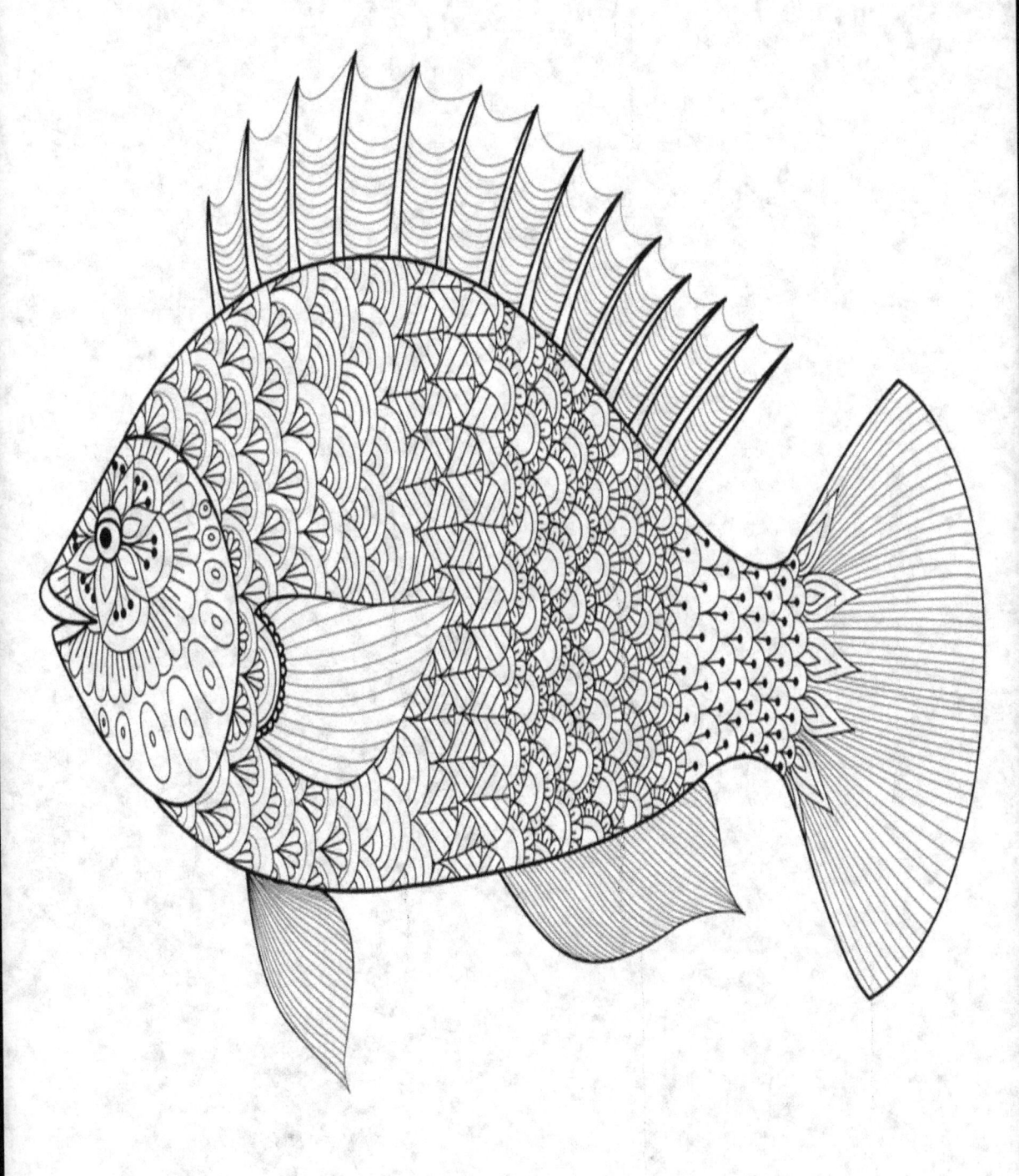

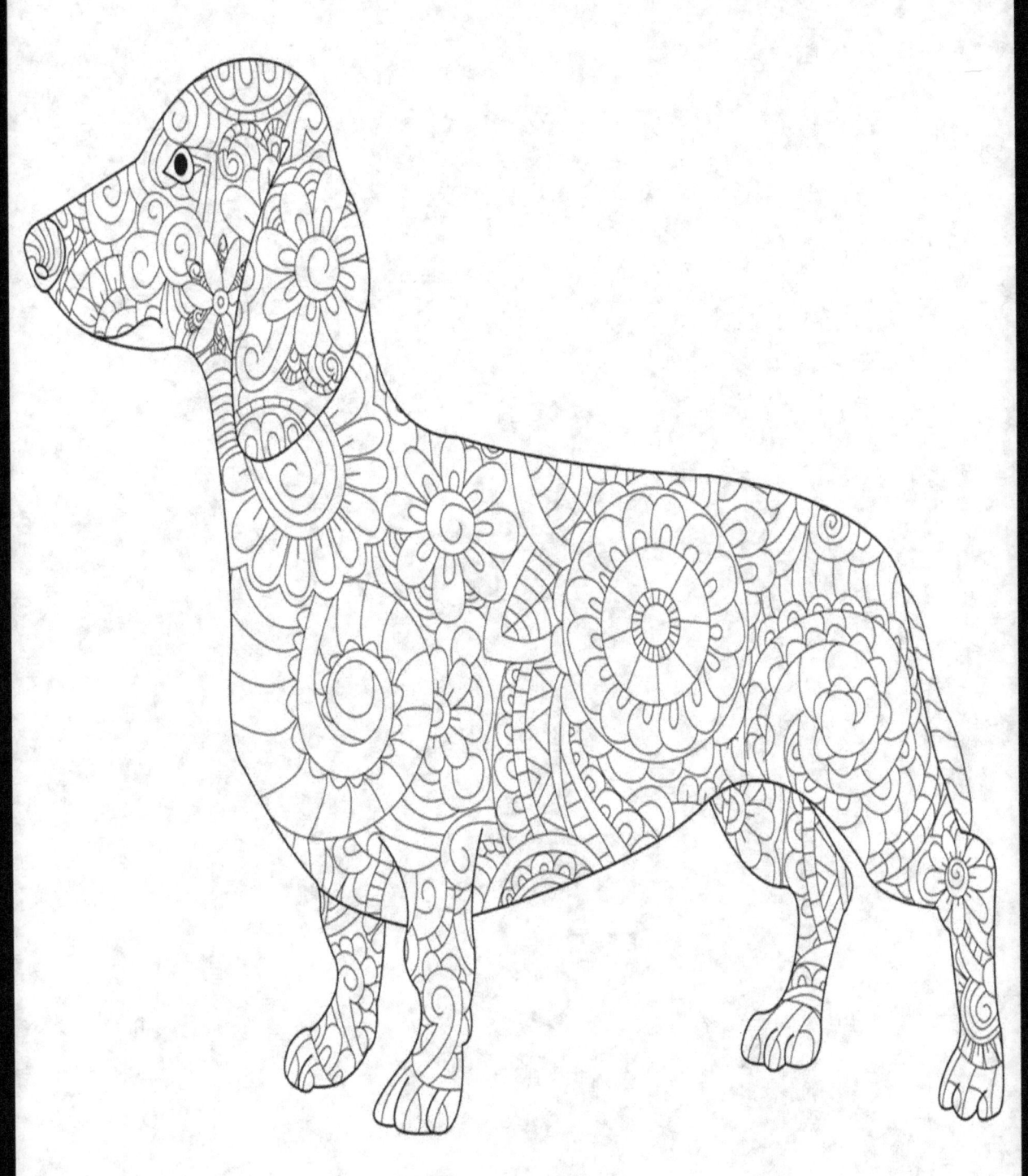

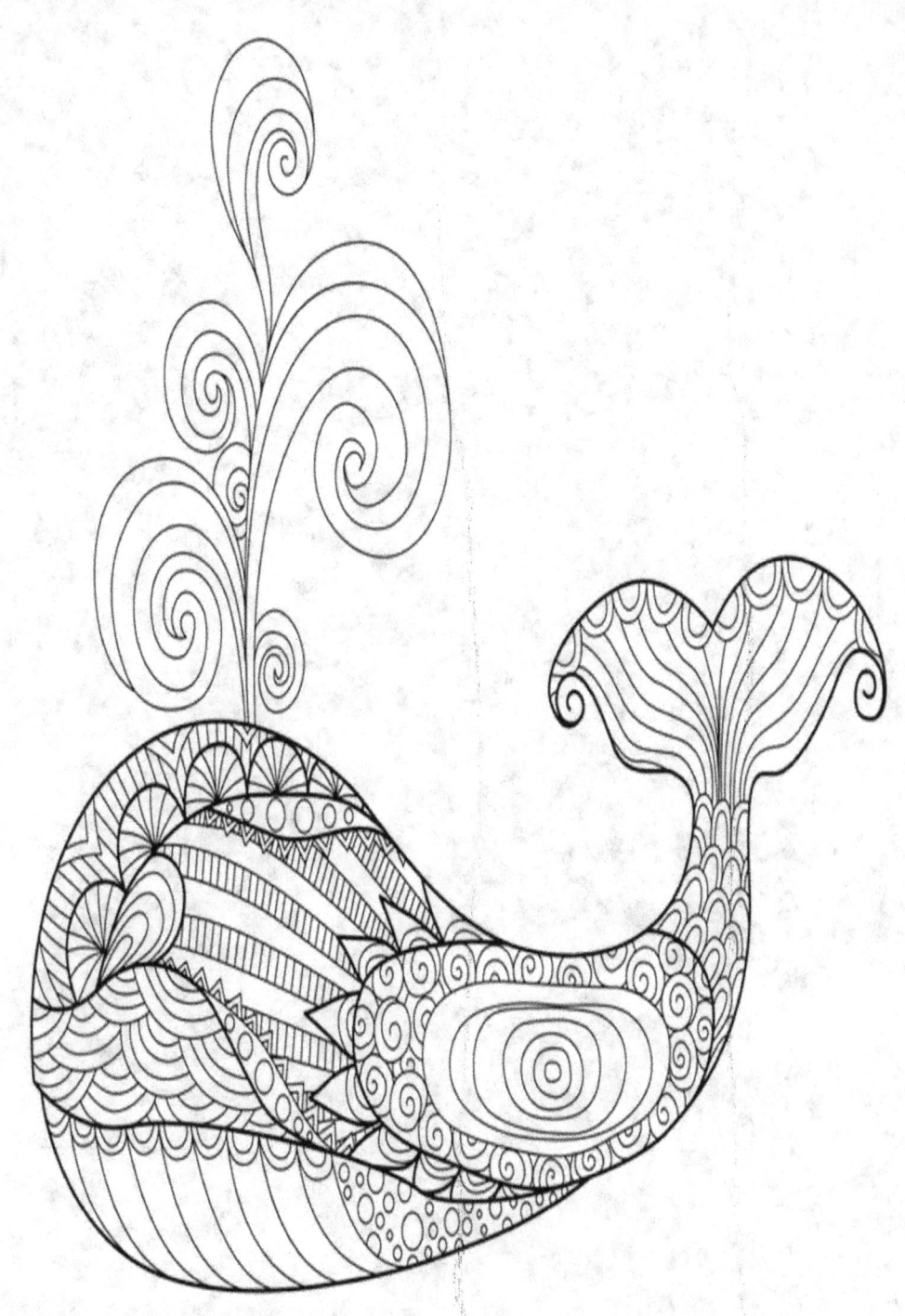

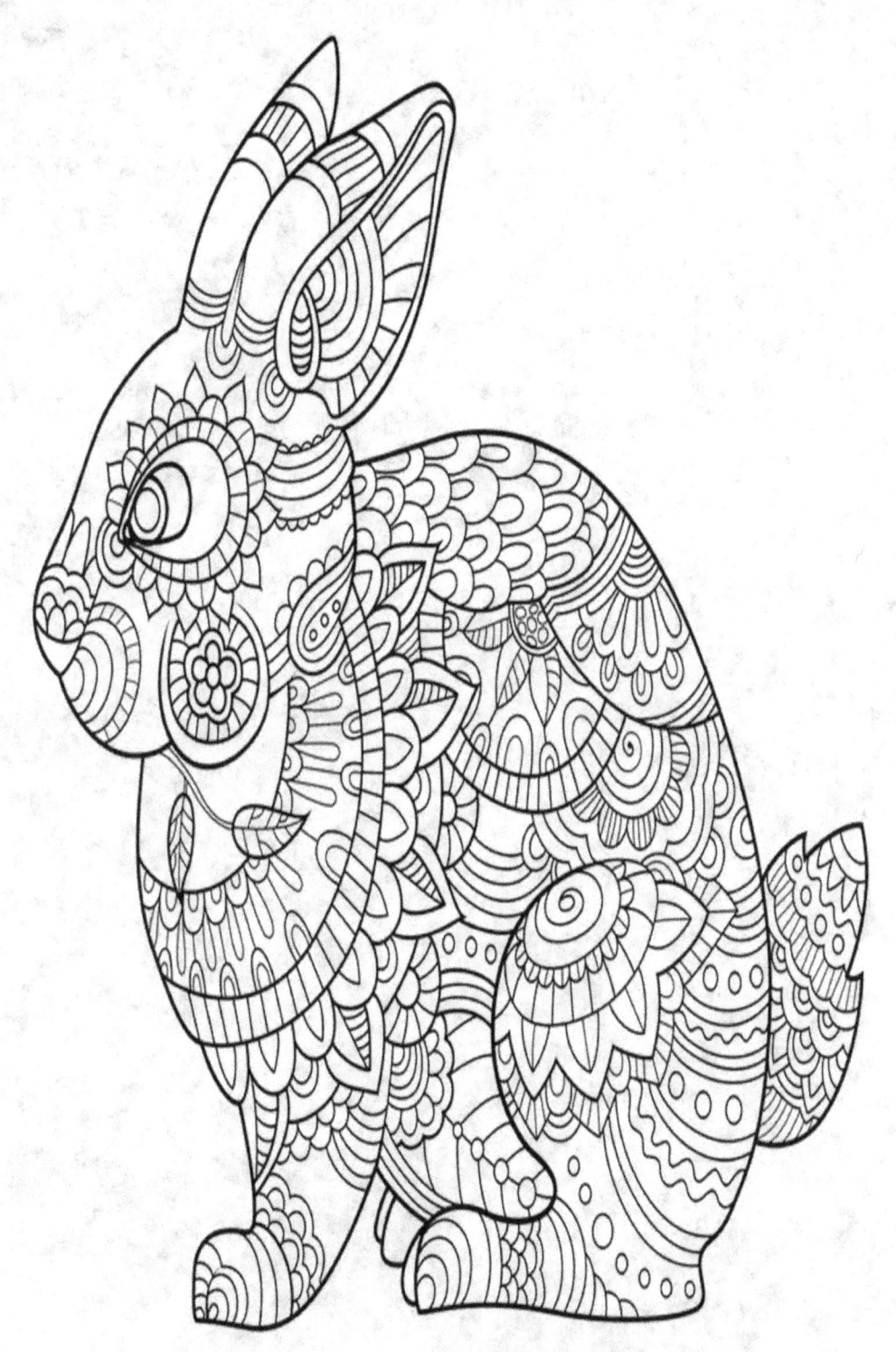

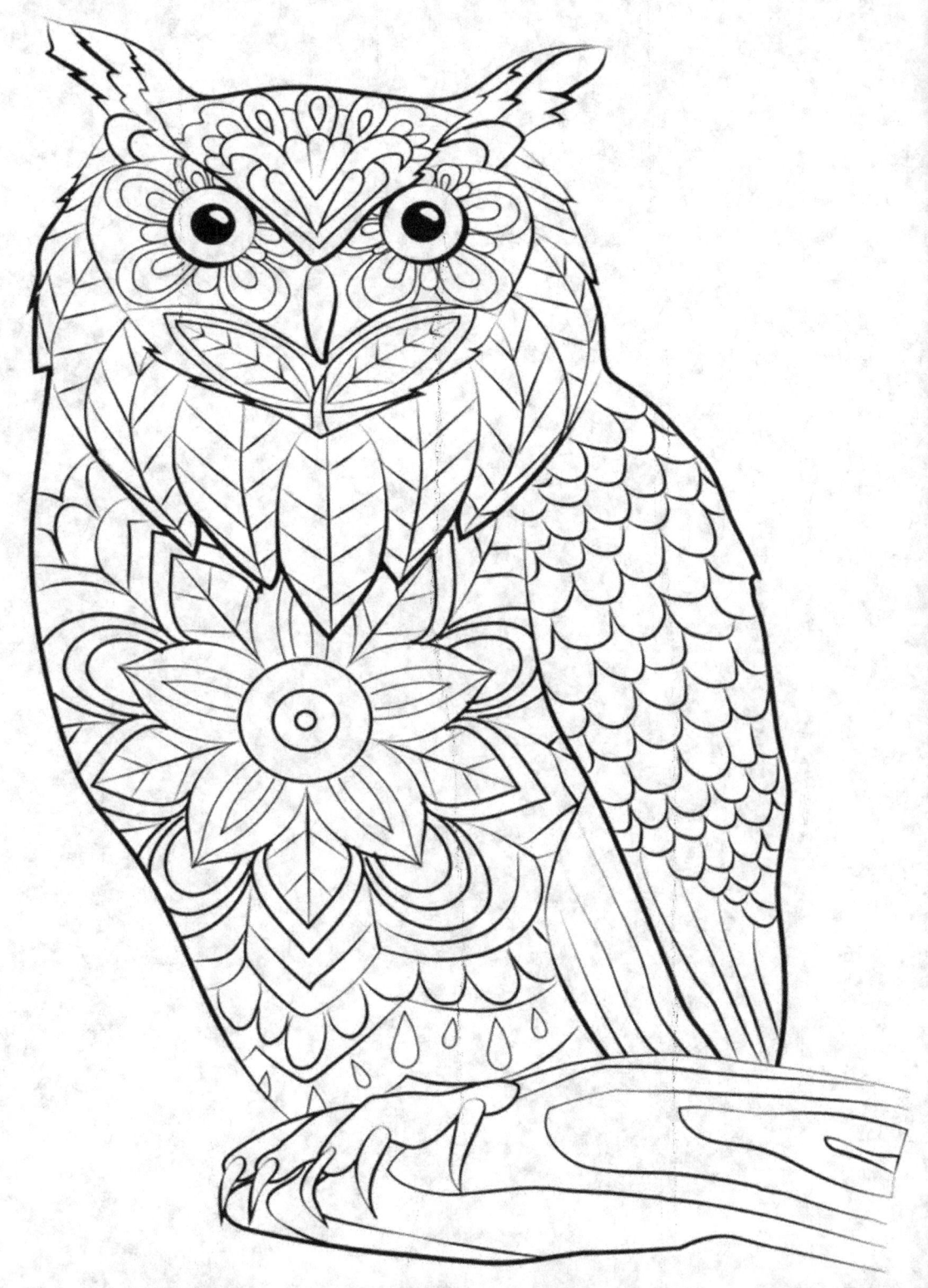

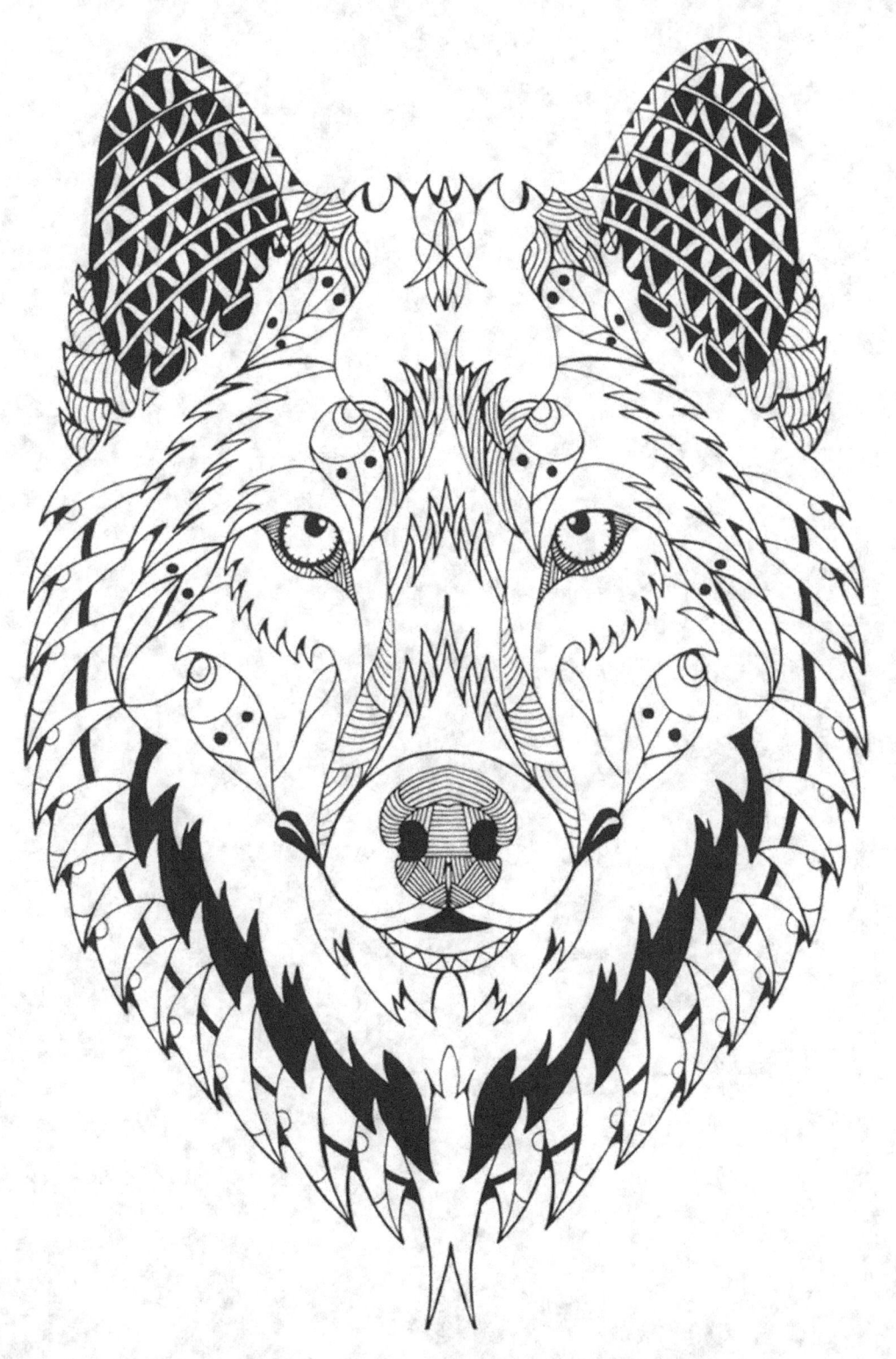

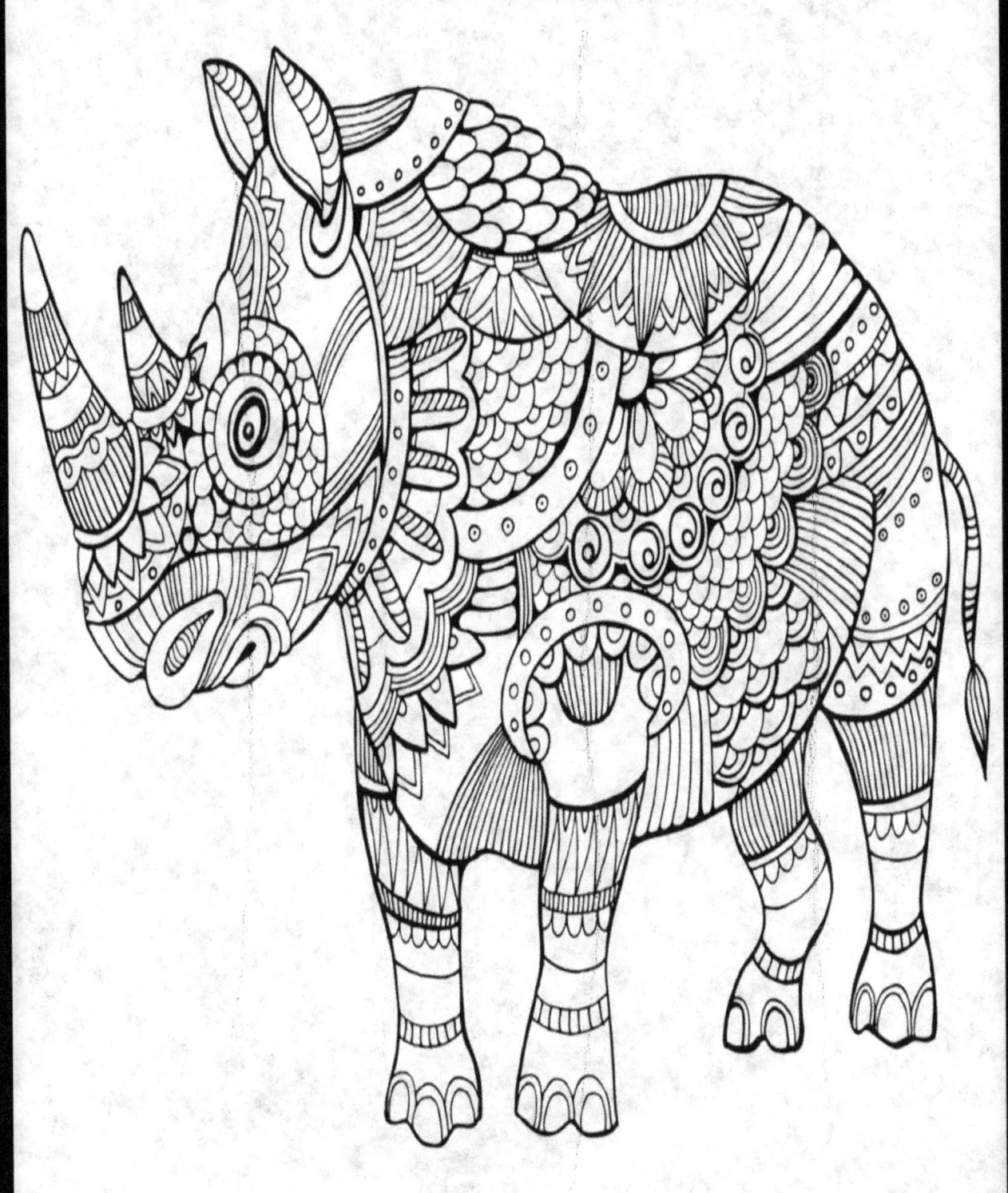

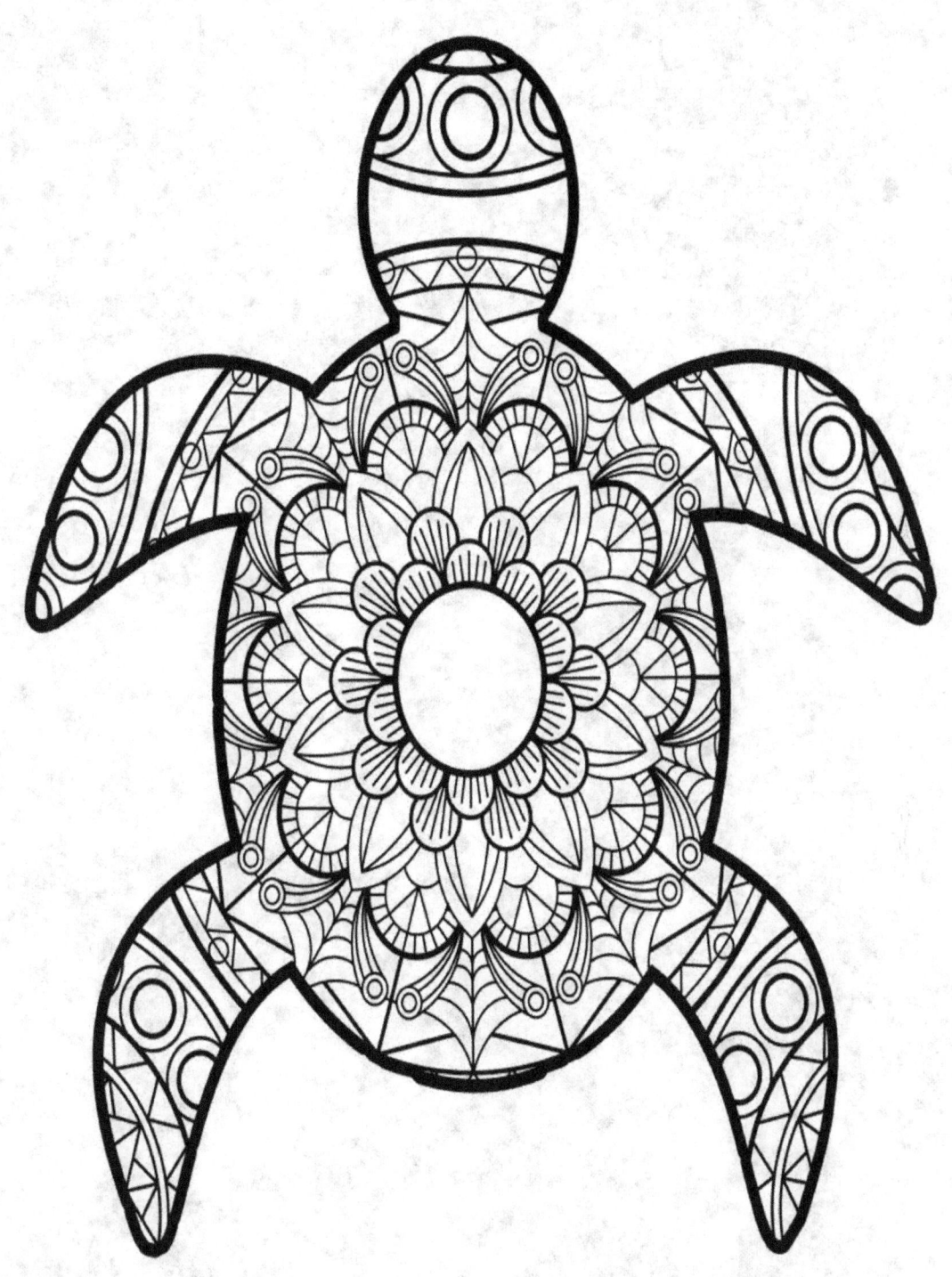

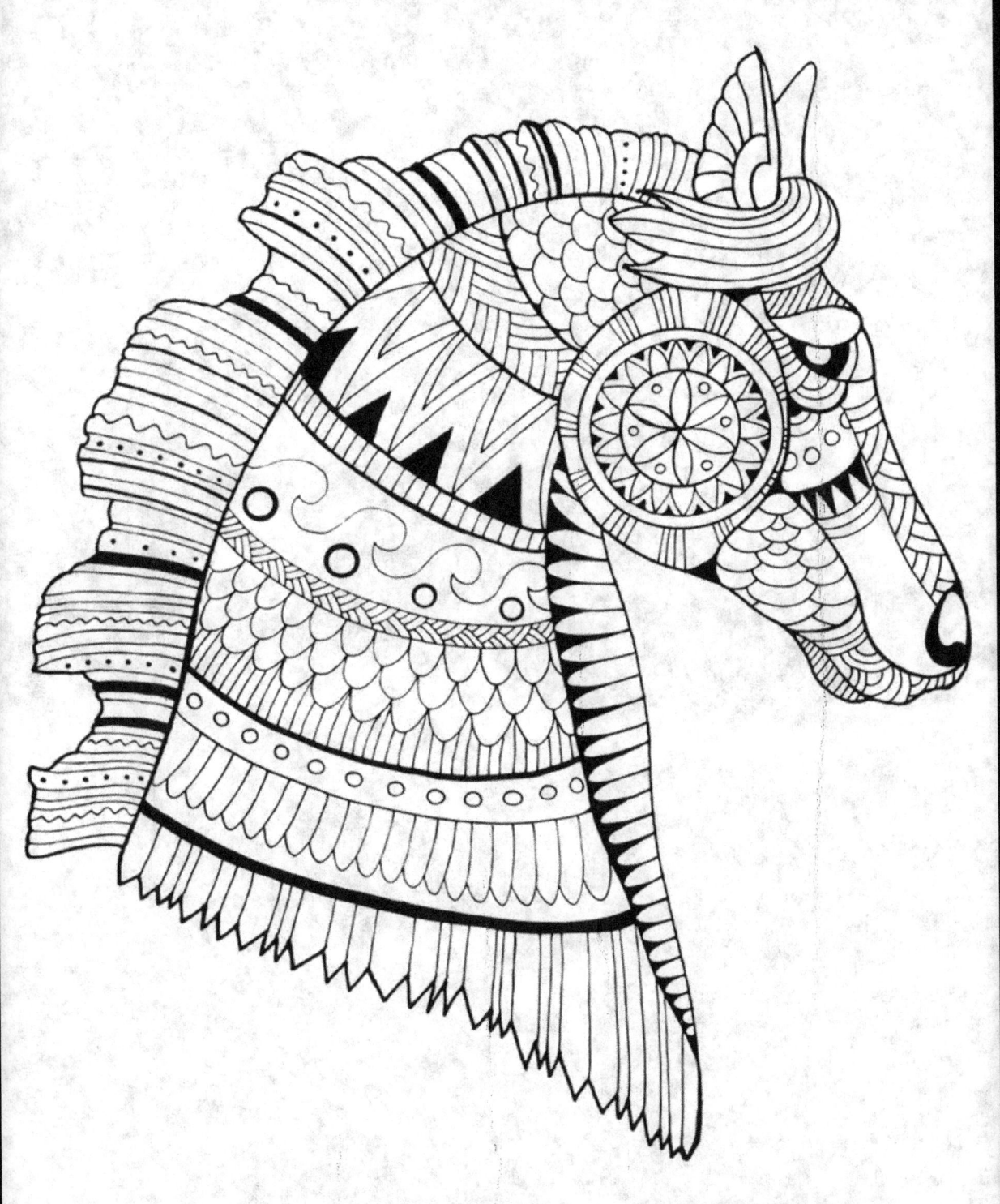

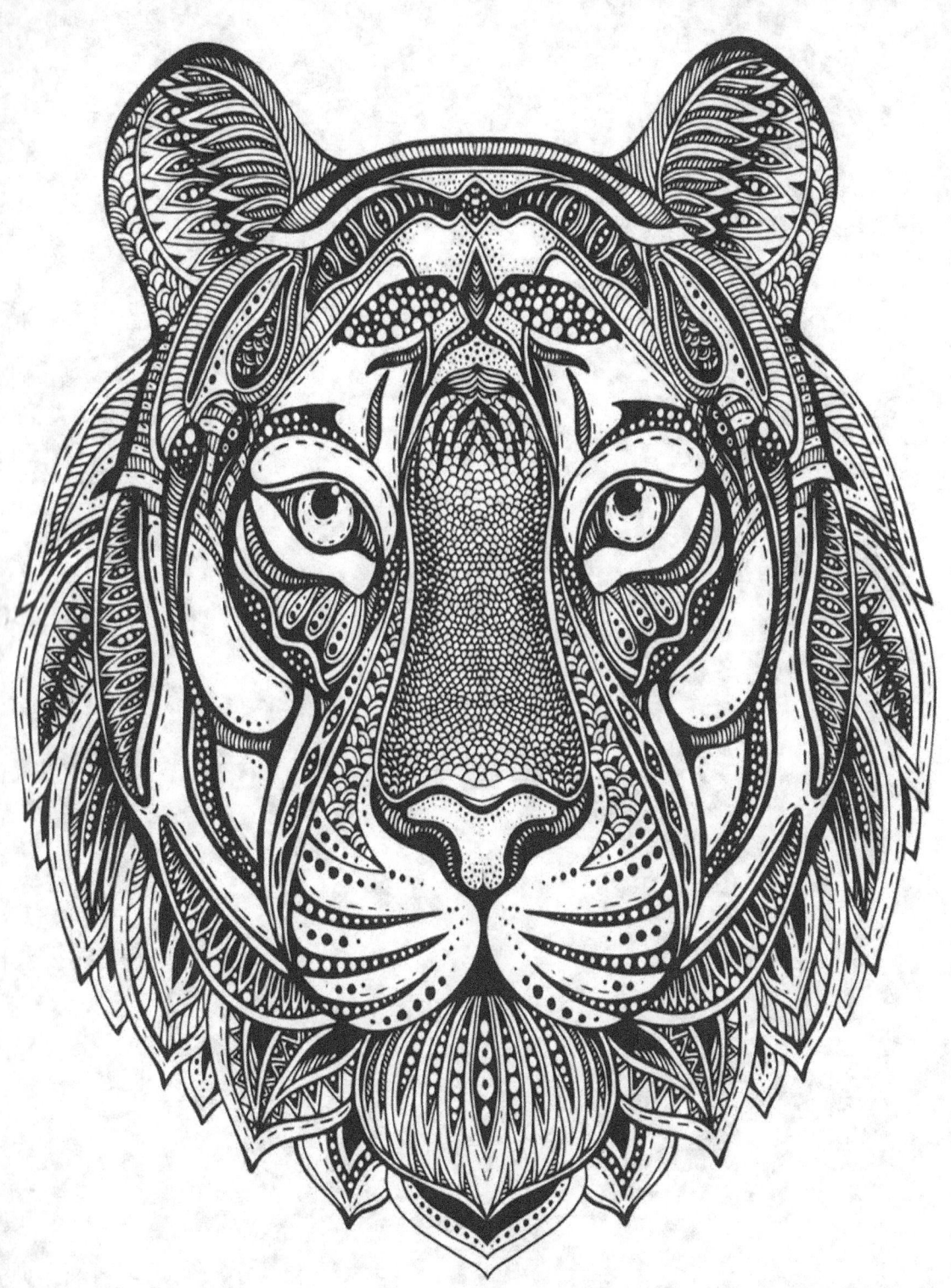

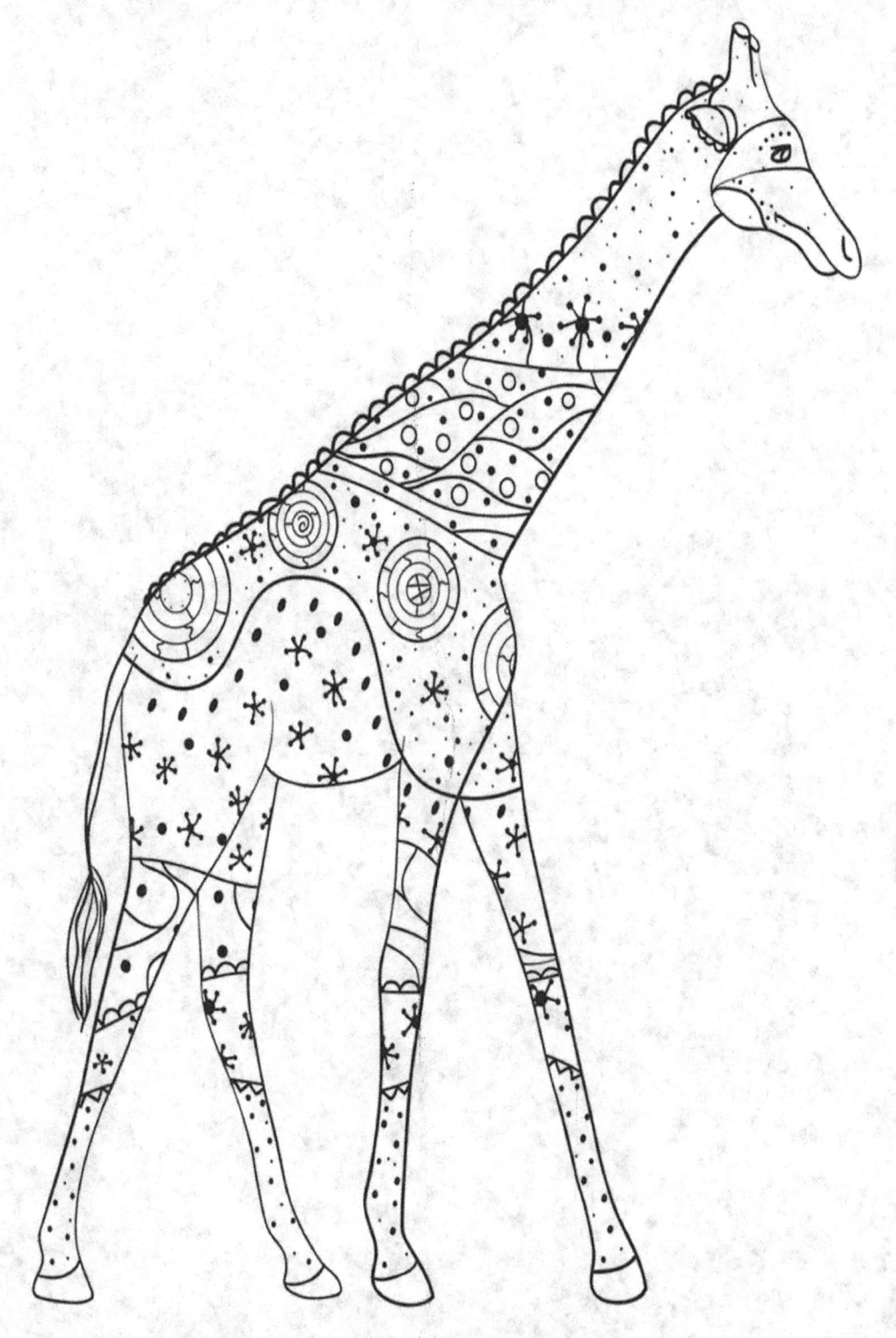

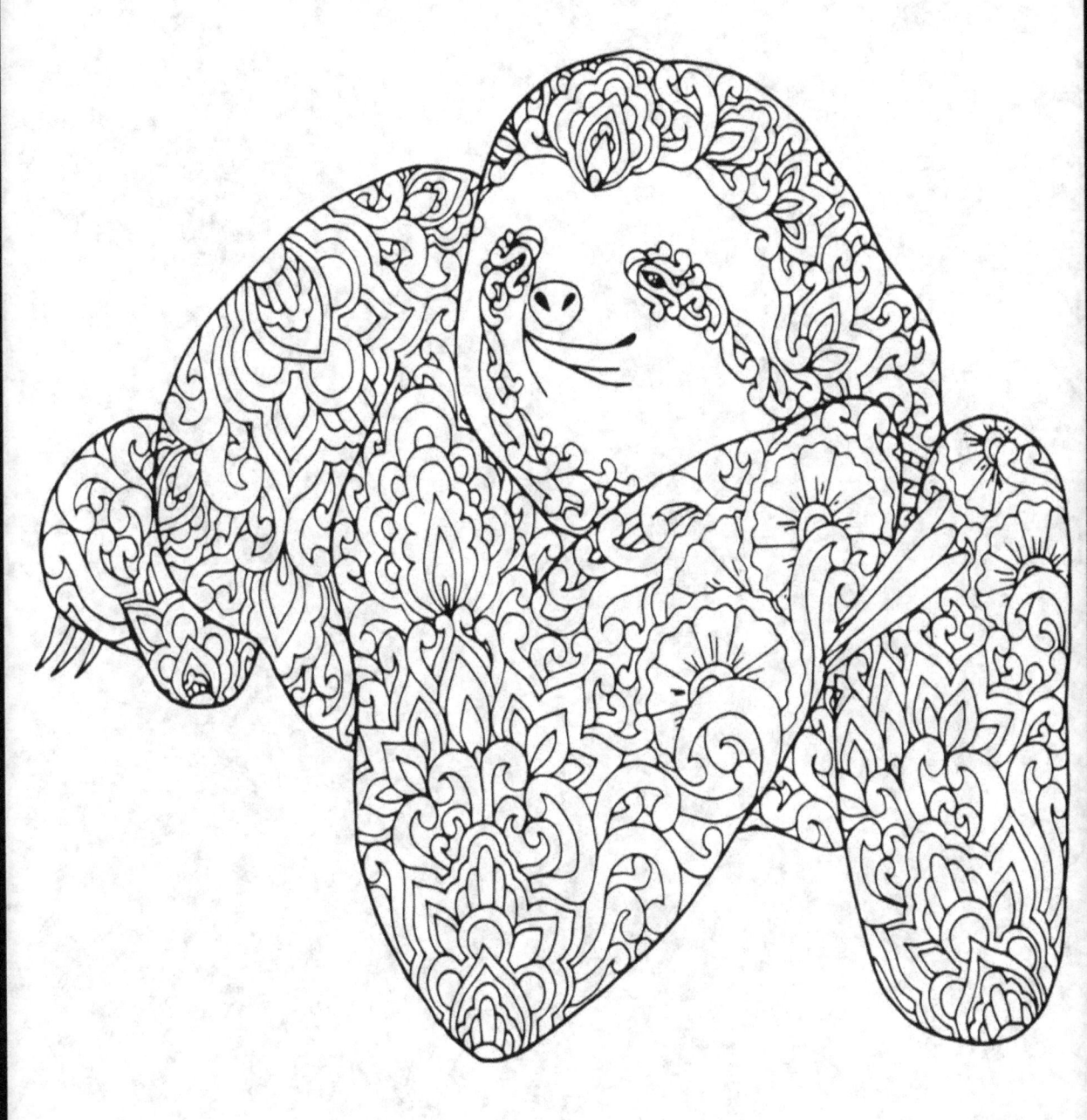

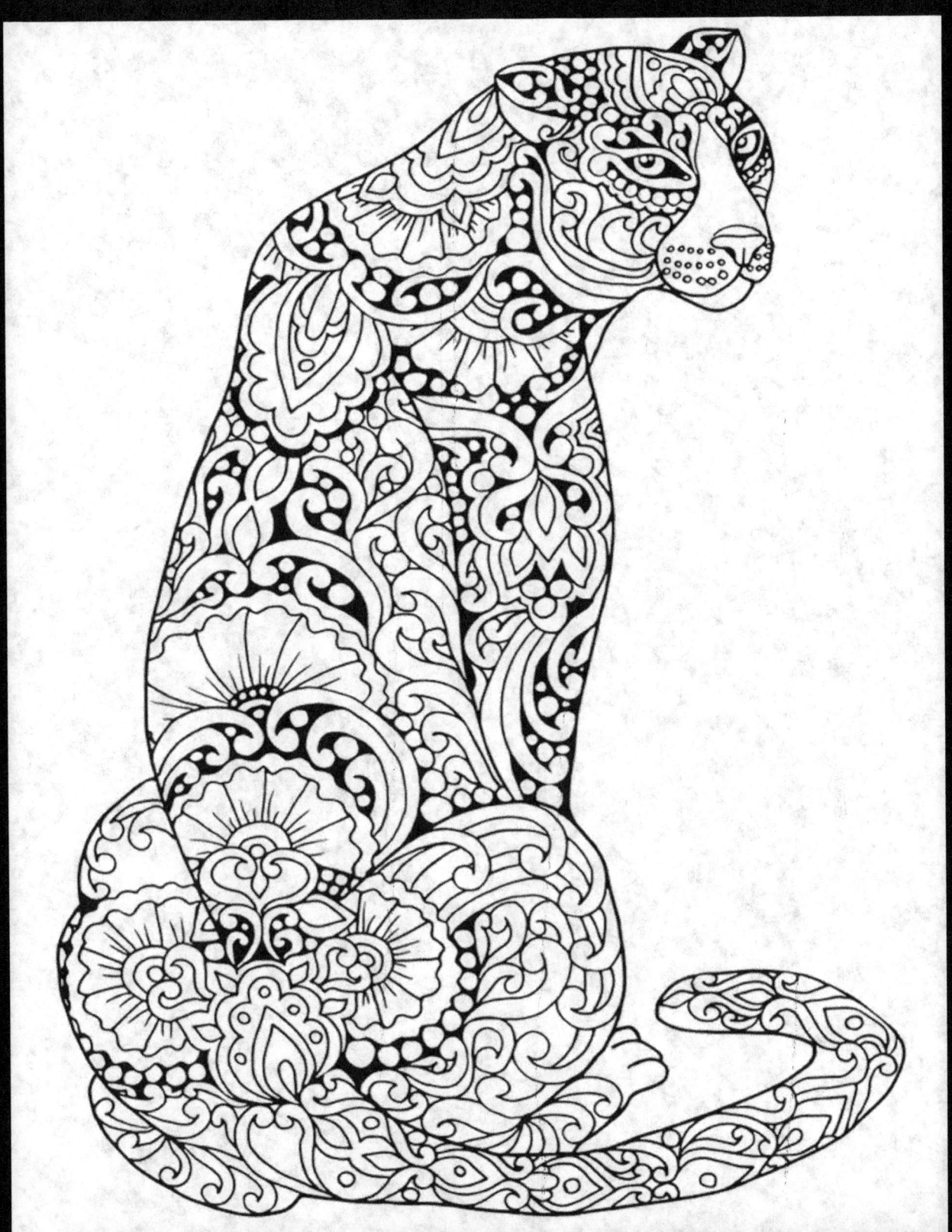

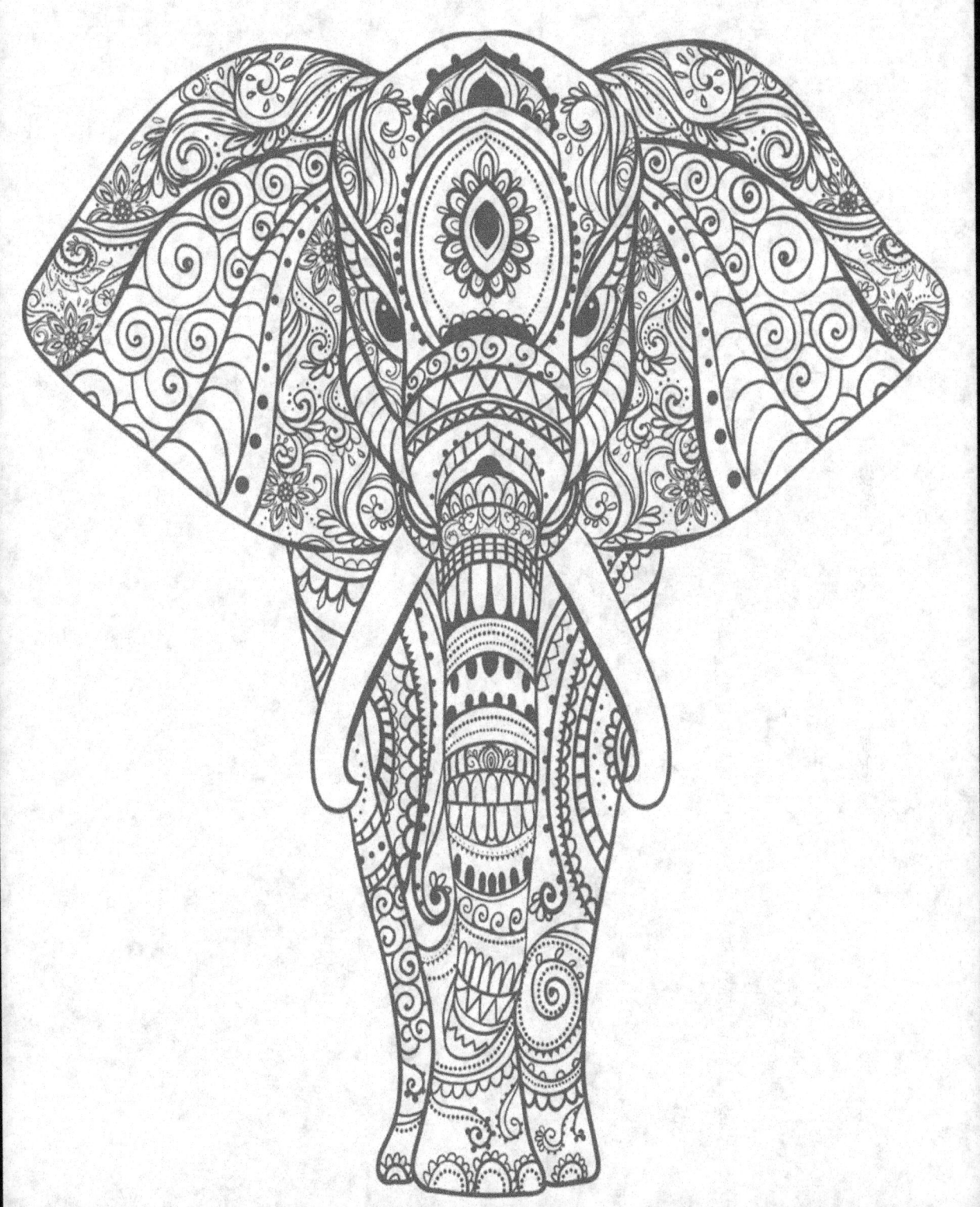

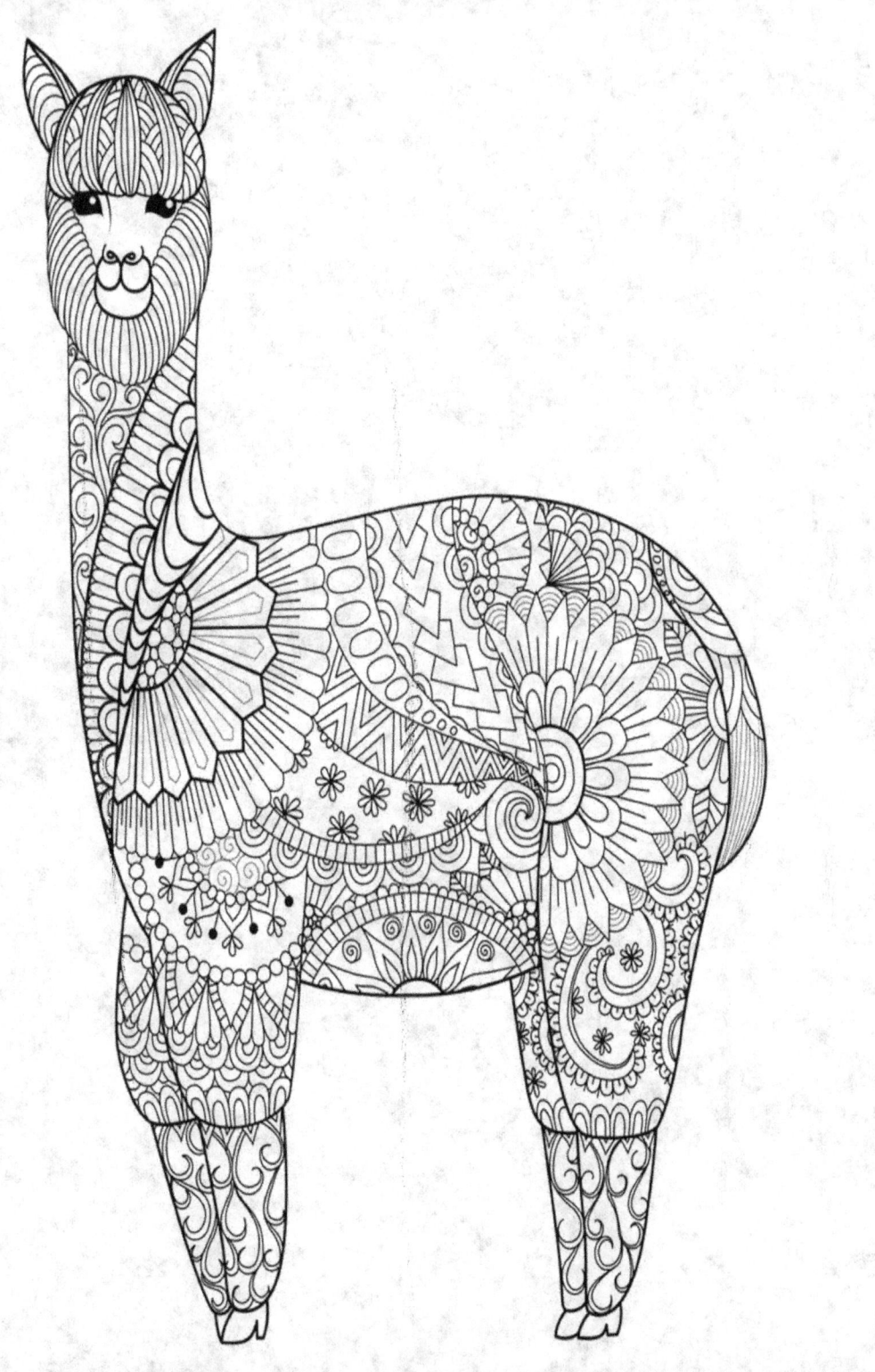

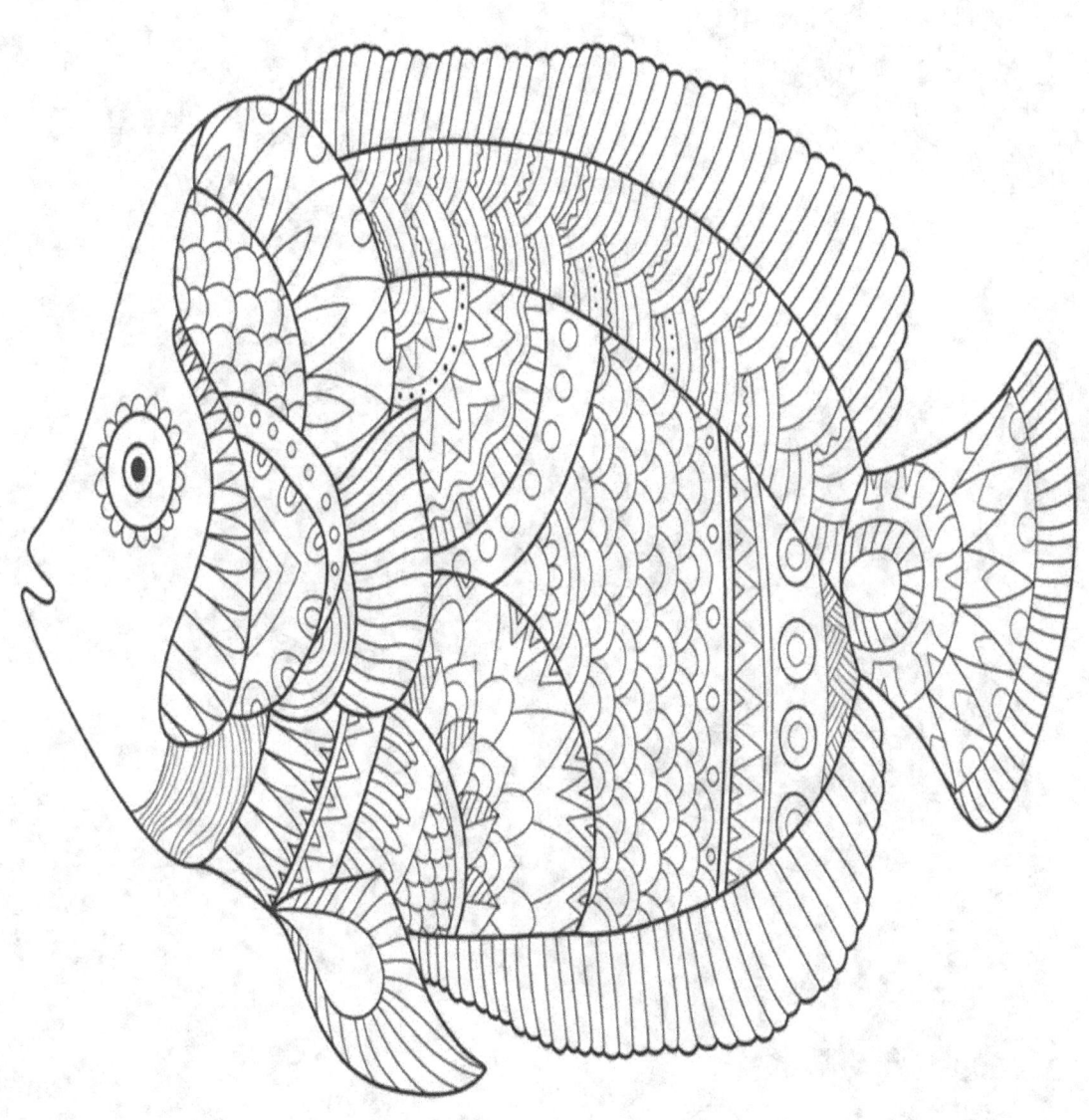

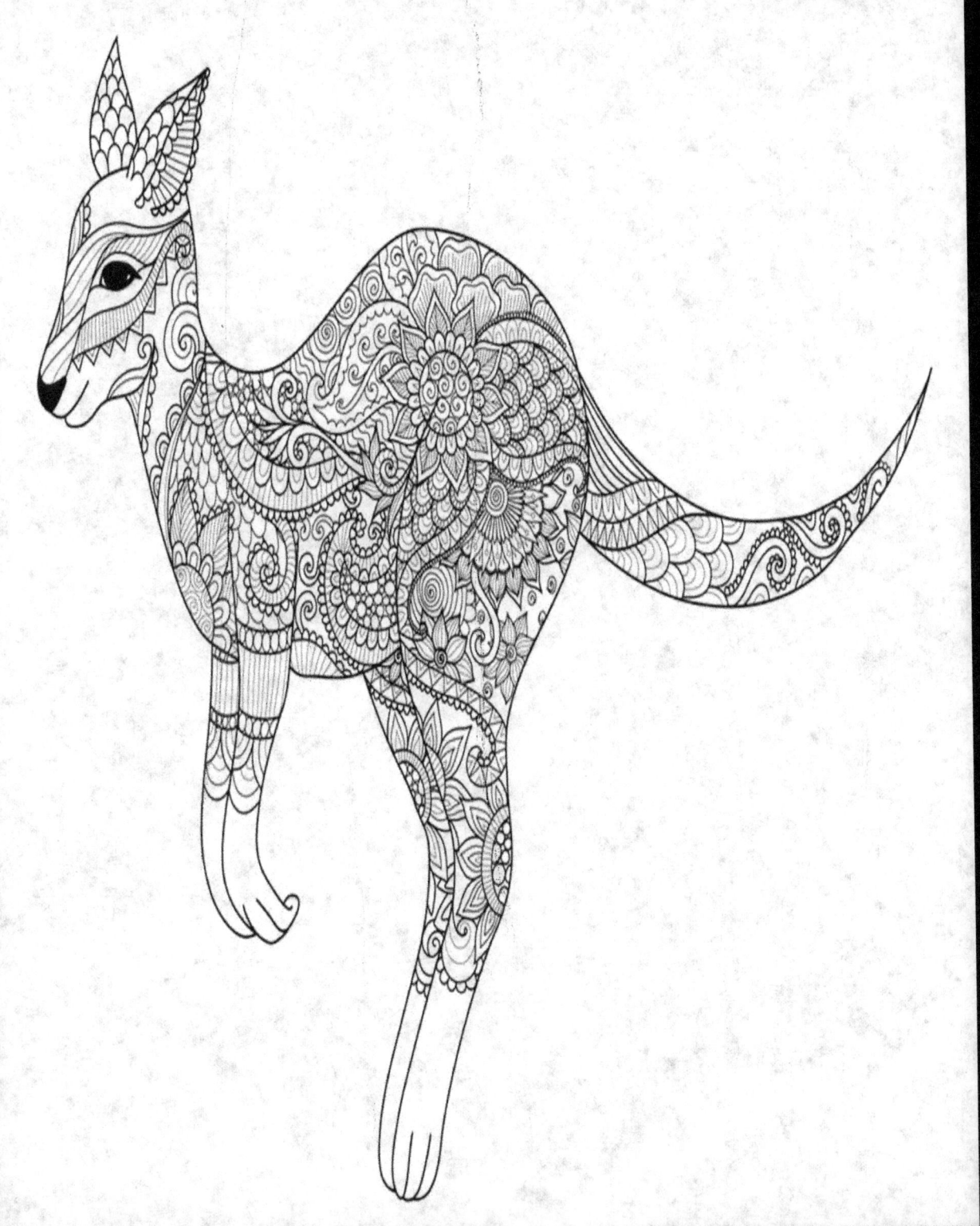

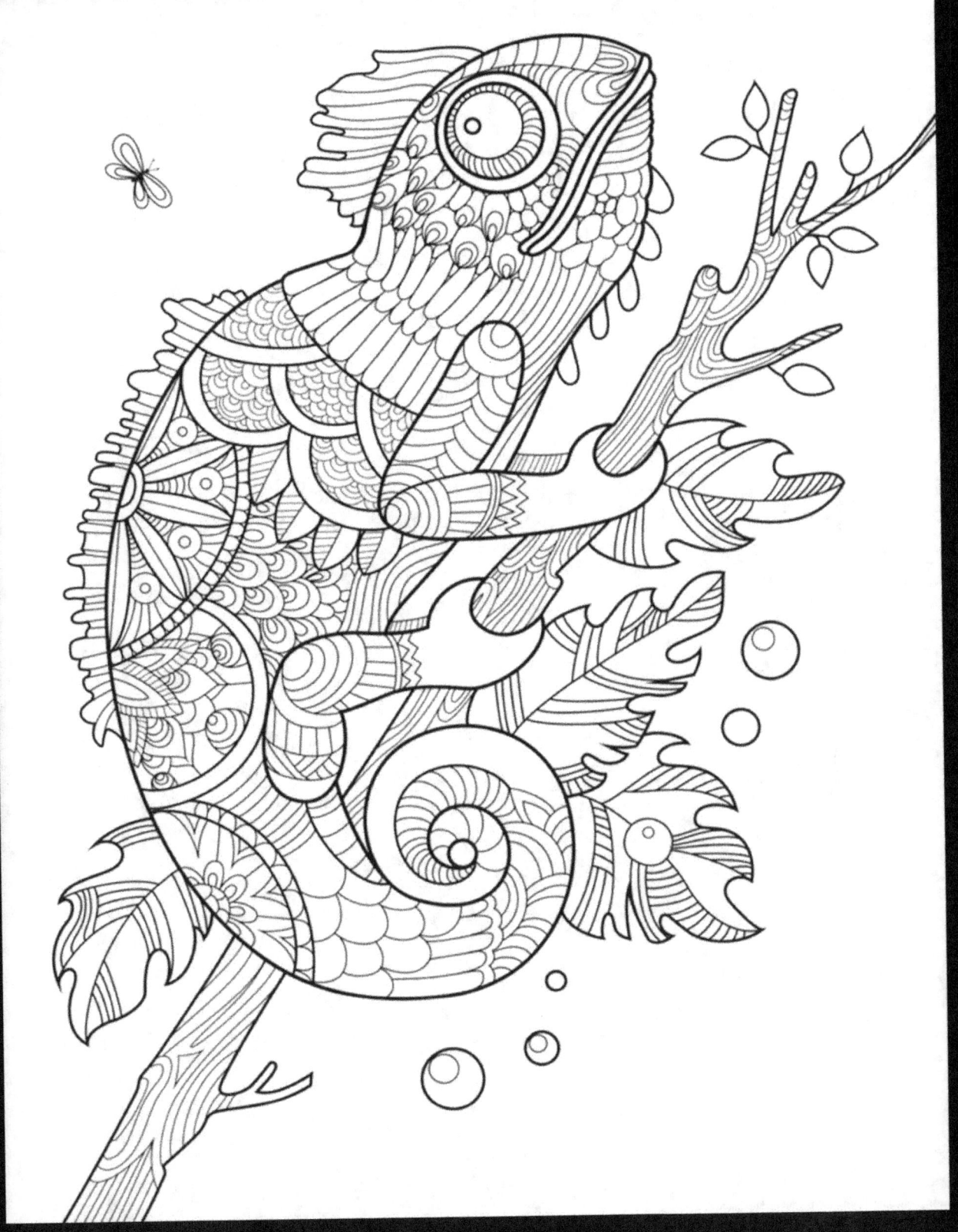

www.ingramcontent.com/pod-product-compliance
Lightning Source LLC
Chambersburg PA
CBHW080506220526
45465CB00006B/2396